Spirit Magic

THE ESSENTIAL
MIND BODY AND SPIRIT BOOKS

Spirit Magic

Rituals, exercises, connection

Sirian Shadow

ROCKPOOL

A Rockpool book
PO Box 252
Summer Hill
NSW 2130
Australia

rockpoolpublishing.com
Follow us! rockpoolpublishing
Tag your images with #rockpoolpublishing

ISBN: 9781922468055

Published in 2026 by Rockpool Publishing

Design and typesetting by Sara Lindberg, Rockpool Publishing
Edited by Jessica Cox

Printed and bound in China
10 9 8 7 6 5 4 3 2 1

Contents

Introduction

Spirit work is not new. It is ancient, deeply rooted, and has shown up in every culture across time under different names and forms. In the modern age, however, spirit work has become something else entirely, something both vast and intimidating. It can feel overwhelming to know where to begin, especially when you're confronted with rigid systems, conflicting beliefs, or gatekeeping from others who claim to know "the right way." If that's what brought you here, know this: you are not alone, and you are already enough.

This book is the second of two complementary, independent volumes. The first offers insight into the unseen world: its histories, energies, and how we might comprehend the beings that inhabit it. It's about building a foundation of knowledge, context, and respect. This book is different. This is the guidebook, the part where knowledge turns into experience. It's where we step from theory into practice. It's about doing the work. But even more than that, this book is an invitation.

I'm not here to give you a doctrine or dogma. I'm not here to tell you what to believe or how to name your practice. Instead, I'm here to show you what has worked for me, and help you uncover what might work for you. My approach to spirit work is intuitive, grounded in experience, and woven with influences from traditions

I've studied and respectfully learned from, but never claimed as my own. You'll find threads from Western esotericism, folk practices, mysticism, animism, and the occult throughout this book. I'm not claiming mastery over them, but I've found value in their teachings and echoes across systems. And in that overlap, I've discovered something real, something powerful, something that works.

That's what I want to share with you: a living, breathing approach to spirit work that evolves with you as you grow. One that empowers you to step into your role as a spirit worker – not someday, not when you've mastered it all, but now.

Rather than following a singular tradition, in this book you'll be invited to explore, experiment, and engage with spirits and spiritual energies in a way that feels right to you. Spirit work isn't a fixed system, it's a relationship. It's a dynamic, evolving dialogue between you and the unseen world. The exercises and techniques shared here are offered to help you build that relationship, deepen your abilities, and develop the confidence to trust your own experience.

Still, I want to clarify something important; spirit work is real. The results are real. The shifts you experience in energy, perception, and your own sense of self are not imagined or pretend. They are the very real effects of stepping into your power and aligning with forces greater than yourself. That is why this book has been structured not just as a manual, but as a rite of passage.

As you read and apply the practices, you are actively becoming. You're stepping into the identity of a practitioner, spirit worker, mystic, whatever title or label feels authentic to you. This book will help you claim your identity as a spirit worker, confidently and unapologetically. You do not need to be initiated into a closed tradition to begin. You do not need permission from anyone to do this work. All you need is reverence, willingness, curiosity, and discernment. With those tools, you're ready.

And if you've ever felt like you didn't quite belong in more rigid spaces, or if you've been made to feel like you're doing it "wrong," know this: there is room for you here. This path is yours to walk. If something in this book resonates, use it. If something doesn't, leave it. That doesn't make it wrong; it simply means it's not yours right now. Spirit work honors personal sovereignty above all else. So take a deep breath. Prepare to listen deeply. Stay grounded. Keep your heart open. And begin.

A NOTE ON SUCCESS IN SPIRIT WORK

Most people who struggle with spirit work aren't lacking ability; they're unwilling to question their own beliefs. True spirit work asks us to set aside rigid ideas, and accept that much of what we've been taught about reality may be incomplete or even wrong. If you cling too tightly to outside opinions, doctrines, or fears, you'll stay stuck in your head instead of opening to real experience.

This path is about discernment, intuition, and your personal truth. Be willing to let your reality shift, release what no longer serves you, and trust your feelings and perceptions. Spirit work is not just copying someone else's formula, but about writing your own. What I share in these pages are tools, methods, and insights that have worked for me. They are not the only way, nor the "right" way, but a map of what is possible. My hope is that you try, experiment, and let your own experience teach you. Spirit work thrives when you step into it with openness and integrity, rather than fear. At its heart, this practice is about empowerment. You are capable of discernment. You are capable of connection. And you are capable of carving your own path with spirits and energies, in a way that is safe, respectful, and uniquely yours.

CHAPTER 1

Sensing spirits

At its core, spirit work is the art of engaging with nonphysical beings and the subtle energies that exist alongside our material reality. It is a living, breathing practice that spans ancient traditions, modern mysticism, personal intuition, and ritual discipline. It is not about perfection, or adhering strictly to one doctrine or dogma; rather, it is about cultivating a deep relationship with the spirit world in a way that is authentic to you.

Many people come to spirit work through curiosity, others through profound personal experiences or spiritual awakenings. Regardless of the entry point, the journey into spirit work is always one of transformation. It reshapes the way you see the world. It deepens your awareness. And when practiced with integrity and clarity, it offers profound insight, healing, and empowerment.

What exactly is "spirit work"? This term means different things to different practitioners, and that's part of what makes it so powerful and sometimes so misunderstood. For some, spirit work is about working with ancestors and guides. For others, it may involve rituals of invocation, petitioning deities, or journeying to other realms. Some people refer to spirit work when they engage with divination, spellwork, or energy healing. In truth, spirit work can include all this and more.

One of the most important things to remember is that spirit work is a relationship, not a one-sided endeavor. Just as we don't build relationships in the physical world by issuing commands and expecting compliance, we shouldn't approach spirit work with entitlement or assumption. Spirit work requires reverence, patience, humility, and clarity. It's as much about listening as speaking. It's about showing up consistently, doing your inner work, and tending to your spiritual hygiene and discernment.

In my own journey, I've worked with spirits as allies, teachers, protectors, and challengers. I've experienced deep healing and uncomfortable truths. I've made mistakes, learned lessons, and been humbled again and again. But through it all, I've seen that this work changes lives. When approached with respect and care, spirit work can bring clarity, empowerment, and a deep sense of purpose.

Before diving into full-on spirit encounters or rituals, however, it's important to build trust with your own senses. You are your own most important tool in this work. If you don't trust what you're feeling or picking up on, it's going to be hard to navigate any interaction with confidence. The first skill every spirit worker must develop is sensitivity. Not everyone will feel or sense spirits in the same way, and not everyone will have intense, cinematic experiences. But everyone – yes, everyone – has the innate ability to perceive spiritual energy. We just need to learn how to listen.

For some, sensing spirits begins with physical sensations: chills down the spine, tingling skin, or pressure changes in the air. Others may feel a shift in mood or emotion when spirits are near. Some people see flashes of light, shadowy forms, or impressions in their mind's eye. You might hear sounds, voices, or feel words forming in your thoughts, which don't feel like your own. There is no "right" way to sense spirits, there is only *your* way.

When you're learning to sense spirits, your physical environment becomes your training ground. Spirits often communicate through environmental shifts, changes in temperature, light, pressure, and even scent. You might suddenly smell something sweet or smoky with no logical explanation. Maybe the air feels denser, or the room becomes unusually quiet, as if something has just shifted. Pay attention to these subtle changes. Don't overthink them, just observe.

BUILD AWARENESS THROUGH STILLNESS

One of the best ways to build this awareness is through stillness. Spend some time each day sitting in silence, either in meditation or quiet reflection. Let your awareness expand beyond your thoughts and into the room around you. This doesn't need to be complicated. You're not trying to "see" anything right away, just feel. What's the atmosphere like? What do you notice about the space when you're not doing anything but being present with it? Rather than trying to force a connection or ask for a sign, simply pay attention. Just like muscles need to be trained for strength, you need to train your spiritual senses through presence and practice. Without this foundational awareness, it becomes easy to mistake imagination, anxiety, or wishful thinking for genuine spirit contact.

Over time, you'll develop what I call your "spiritual baseline," an inner sense of how energy normally feels in your space and in your body. Once you know your baseline, it becomes easier to notice when something new enters the picture. It's like suddenly hearing a new instrument in a song you've listened to a hundred times. You may not know what it is right away, but you'll know something is different. The truth is, most of us are already sensing spirits, we've just been trained to tune them out. We're told it's just our imagination, or that we're being dramatic. But intuition is rarely loud. It speaks in whispers, nudges, flickers at the edge of your awareness. The more you listen, the louder it gets.

Perhaps one of the most important lessons in sensing spirits is learning to trust yourself. Your intuition is the compass that will guide you through the unknown. It doesn't speak loudly, it whispers. At times, it may feel like your imagination, but the more you engage with it, the more distinct it becomes. You might receive images, feelings, or knowings that don't come from your logical mind. With practice, you'll be able to distinguish between wishful thinking, fear-based reactions, and true intuitive insight. This takes time and patience but remember: every single practitioner, no matter how experienced, once stood where you are now.

It's also important to stay embodied during this process. Spirit work isn't about floating away or disconnecting from the physical. The body is one of your greatest tools in this work. Your nervous system often picks up on subtle shifts in energy first. You might feel a chill, a sudden warmth, or even a buzzing sensation across your skin. These are not random, they're signals. Learning how your body speaks to you is key to building confidence in your spiritual senses. If you're unsure whether something is spiritual or imagined, go back to your body. Ask yourself: *Does this feel familiar? Does it carry emotion? Is it coming from outside of me or within?* Sometimes you'll find the answer in your gut before you form the question in your mind.

As you open yourself to sensing spirits, one of the simplest and most powerful things you can do is create a ritual space. This doesn't need to be elaborate. It can be as simple as lighting a candle and taking a few deep breaths to set your intention. Speak aloud: "*I'm open to connecting with spirit in a way that is safe, clear, and aligned with my highest good.*" Your intention sets the frequency. It tells the spirit world what kind of contact you're available for.

Over time, you'll notice that certain spirits show up more often, or that you feel drawn to particular types of energy. This is part of forming your personal relationship with the spirit world. Keep a journal. Record your impressions, even if they seem small. This helps you track your growth and reinforces trust in your experience.

As you begin sensing spirit, remember: you are in control. You are not required to open the door to every energy that knocks. Just like in the physical world, not everyone who wants your attention deserves your attention. Part of being a spirit worker is understanding that this work is built on mutual respect, clear boundaries, and personal sovereignty. You have the right to say, "Not now," set times and conditions, and demand clarity or alignment from the spirits you interact with. Spirits will often mirror your energy. The more you show up with focus, clarity, and respect, the more refined and powerful your interactions will become.

PRACTICE SUMMARY

- Spend 5 minutes each day in silence, noticing subtle sensations in your environment: temperature shifts, tingling, or pressure.
- Keep a journal of these impressions and how they change in different settings.
- Try sitting in a place you already know feels "energetic" (such as a forest, old building, or sacred site) and record what stands out.

CHAPTER 2

Development and attuning

When you begin to attune yourself to invisible energies, it's incredibly important to be gentle with yourself. Forcefulness will only cause damage, and walking the spiritual path must be a lifelong commitment. Don't rush yourself if you aren't immediately seeing the results you hoped for. Force and frustration, just like fear, will only lead to blockages, low vibrations, and channeling negative entities. Don't be afraid of intuitive development; instead, proceed with care. Everyone is capable of the intuitive development to work with energies. Everyone experiences intuitive messages consciously or unconsciously; the trick is to start paying attention. If you're having trouble differentiating between logic, imagination, or intuition, try practicing intuitive analysis.

Intuition is a mixture of understanding your instincts combined with receiving information from the senses. When you follow this information or message that your body tells you is true and you trust it, you gain an inner sense of knowing. This knowledge, combined with an activated third eye, is what practitioners utilize to hear and communicate with spirits. Psychics and mediums use it for channeling; magicians and witches use it in magic. It's a practical skill to implement with energy and spirit work.

Furthermore, psychic and intuitive development is all a matter of balance. Just as it takes work and dedication to perfect skills or techniques, forcing yourself to become great can also be harmful. Think of a bodybuilder: if she doesn't give herself enough time to recuperate or rest, she could harm her body from fatigue, broken-down muscles, and being overworked. She needs to allow for rest and recuperation to give the body time to rebuild and improve. The same is true for energy workers. Remember to practice and dedicate yourself, but don't overdo it. Allow for the flow of energy to occur instead of trying to force it, and you'll see much more positive results.

To tune into unseen energies, practitioners use many different techniques that they've practiced over time, like building muscles. They have often developed their abilities through forms of meditation or trance work and start by using exercises intended to help prepare the individual for meditation. Centering techniques are designed to take your mind off the ordinary waking state and into a deep relaxation state. Often mistaken for meditation, centering is a much more quick and simple practice. Meditation does not happen until the mind has entered a state of inner stillness or silence, or has experienced emptiness called the void.

You may have heard the term "clear your mind," and in some cases, this phrase can be beneficial. But what we actually need to do is begin with centering, which is a practice of focus and understanding how to be present to strengthen clarity. Although each tradition will carry its own version and definition of what centering is, simply put, centering is to direct your focus and either visualize energy so you can begin to utilize it or create the environment required for spiritual communication. This does not indicate that your mind is altogether empty or cleared. In this instance, the practitioner's goal is to remove distraction and form a foundation for energy work. Centering is a primary step in spirit communication and in the work. It's necessary to create a space for clear spirit communication and allow a receptive flow of energy. Centering is simple enough, and in this book, I'll give step-by-step instructions to achieve it by focusing on the breath (see Chapter 7).

Once you can experience your environment with all your senses, you will develop the tools needed for spirit work. Some practices relate centering to mindfulness, in which you focus on being intensely aware of what you're sensing and feeling in the moment, without interpretation or judgment. Practicing mindfulness can involve breathing methods, visualizations, and other practices to relax the body and mind. Some can easily shut out our busy world; others will find it challenging to slow down and notice things. For them, practice is vital.

Before you're ready to practice things like intuitive analysis, centering, or meditation, keep in mind that thoughts will enter. Allow for the flow of thoughts to come and go. Do not hang onto them; notice them and let them leave your mind's eye. This encourages the flow of energy and strengthens the practice of embracing meditative states instead of combating whatever comes into your mind. This is why meditation can be difficult for many, we try too hard to silence and clear all the mind's chatter when really all we want to do is be in the present. Understanding that thoughts come and go will allow for a flow of energy so we can decipher what is of our internal consciousness and what is coming from external sources.

EXERCISE: Intuitive analysis

Whenever you have a choice to make, find a place where you feel comfortable and removed from distraction.

1. **Appreciate and focus on the beauty around you.** This can be literal beauty in nature, such as the reflection of the sun on water, or the beauty you see in your

environment. I once saw beauty in the structure of my bookshelf being categorized and orderly.

2. **Concentrate on your breathing.** Ask yourself: *What option will align me with my highest purpose or what decision is best for me?*

3. **Don't search for the answer.** Instead, wait and listen for words, phrases, or images that come into your mind. Take note of them. There may be a flood of information or just a trickle. Notice which one feels truer and more aligned to your heart.

4. **Lean into the option that just feels absolute.** Place your logical mind aside and learn to listen to that feeling of knowing it's the right choice. In life, you are often presented with guidance in the form of whispers, signs, and synchronicities for the best-case scenario and outcome. Your first instinct is usually correct.

Allow yourself to trust your instincts and what your body tells you. Pondering choices with your mind is the opposite of what we're doing. Listen to how you feel, regardless of if you understand it. This is the beginning of learning to trust your intuition, by how you feel rather than what you think.

PRACTICE SUMMARY

- Begin with short daily meditations to clear your mind and strengthen focus.
- Practice steady breathwork to ground your energy before any spirit work.
- Keep a journal of impressions after each practice session to notice subtle changes.
- At the end of each week, reflect on your progress and note what feels stronger in your perception.

CHAPTER 3

The importance of consent

Developing intuition and connecting with your higher self is critical in spirit work because spirits can communicate in many ways. In Western traditions and culture, we're often taught to apply logic and science to prove scenarios. Spirituality exists outside of measuring with our minds. The answers can be explained, but not by this way of thinking. Give yourself permission to listen to how you feel, and use all your other senses rather than leading with the logical mind. In spirit work, the logical mind can limit your connections. It begins with reconditioning how you think. If you have already developed your intuition and can listen to your heart over your head, you are a step ahead.

Permission and consent are important for practitioners in reconditioning what we believe and how they think so we can be open to spiritual relationships. Anytime the intention of making contact with a spirit is sought, we must begin by giving them permission to manifest.

HOW TO GIVE CONSENT

Giving permission is simple enough: clearly state your intentions out loud to make contact with a spirit. When you give permission, also address them so you are 100 percent aware of who the spirit is that you're giving consent to. If you don't know who the spirit is, you can make more general statements such as:

"I wish to contact my spirit guides of the highest love and compassion, or I wish to speak to my paternal/maternal ancestors who love and protect me."

For the next exercise, we'll begin making contact by administering consent for your spirit guides. Our spiritual allies are always with us: these entities work with us for our benefit. More specifically, spirit guides are among our allies and are the best to begin contacting because they are benevolent, nonphysical entities who have our best interests at heart. They are sanctioned to help us achieve our true will. They are assigned by your higher self before birth and are invested to assist you on your life's journey and development. The length of time your spirit guides spend with you may differ. They may be with you for your entire life, or just a short period of time, like helping you through a particular moment or with a life lesson.

I like to think of them as an invisible team of life coaches, mentors, and counselors. For this reason, it's best to begin spirit work and develop your intuitive or psychic senses by tuning in with your spirit guides.

EXERCISE: Administering consent

Find a comfortable space without any distractions. If you have access to a speaker, play 963 Hz Solfeggio frequency. You can find 963 Hz sounds on YouTube and popular music streaming channels. Simply choose one to your liking and play it while you perform this exercise. This frequency is associated with awakening intuition and activating the pineal gland. It awakens our crown energy center and raises the positive energy and vibrations so we can better connect and establish permission. Listen to this frequency as you meditate. Visualize a bright light, as bright as the sun radiating love and protection above you. Don't worry if your visualization skills aren't perfect; imagining this light is enough to be effective. Visualize the light emanating and flowing down from the top of your head through your crown energy center. Allow it to rest in your heart space, surrounding you in protective energy. Once you are ready, with your eyes closed and feeling a state of calmness and clarity, mentally or verbally call out to your spirit guides:

> *"I wish to connect with and open communication with my spirit guides of the highest truth and compassion."*
>
> *"Spirit guides, I ask you to manifest yourselves to me."*

"I am ready to receive your guidance."

"I want to have a relationship with you."

"I allow you to become a part of my life."

"I am grateful for your love, for your guidance, and for the clarity you provide me with."

As you speak these words of power, keep your eyes closed and let visions enter your mind. You may see images or sounds come closer to you in your mind's eye. Just allow thoughts to come and go. Recognize and notice any thoughts that might enter your mind, but do not follow them. Simply focus on your breath and let them pass. As you remain in this receptive state, pay attention to any images, conversations, words, or sounds that occur. You may hear things in your own voice or from someone unrecognizable; witness them without forcing. Pay attention to your senses. What do you hear? What do you notice? There may be messages provided to you.

This may take one or several tries before you receive confirmation from your guides. It doesn't matter so much if you have a particularly strong bond or relationship with your spirit guides at that time. Your connection will grow stronger as you build your relationship with them and open up more to receive their messages. The key is that you practice administering this consent and state your intentions. Allowing spirit allies to be a part of your life is achieved through communicating permission. Essentially, by setting your intentions through consent you are establishing a spiritual contract, or boundaries, to allow them to manifest and come to your aid in exchange for a relationship with you. These boundaries are fixed; I have never required spiritual protection when my intentions are working for my highest good and the highest good of others. Be assured this is a safe practice.

PRACTICE SUMMARY

- Before beginning any practice, set a spoken boundary: "Only benevolent, respectful spirits are welcome here."
- Experiment with creating energetic "yes/no" signals in your body (such as a tingling in the hand or pressure in the chest) to test spirit consent.
- Journal any experiences where boundaries were respected or crossed, and reflect on what could be done differently.
- Practice withdrawing your energy and closing a session firmly to signal completion.

CHAPTER 4

Balancing intentions

One of the first things people ask when they begin spirit work is: "How do I know if a spirit is good or bad?" It's a valid concern, especially for those who've absorbed years of fear-based conditioning from movies, religious teachings, or sensationalized ghost stories. The truth is, this binary view of spirits as either light or dark, good or evil, is overly simplistic. Spirits, like people, are complex. They operate across a spectrum, not inside a box.

Overcoming spiritual bias

Spiritual bias is something most of us carry without even realizing it. We inherit beliefs from our culture, family, and spiritual communities. For example, the idea that angels are always benevolent and demons are always malevolent has been reinforced through centuries of doctrine. But when you step outside of religious frameworks and view these beings energetically, things get more nuanced.

Real spiritual work invites you to look deeper. Not all challenging spirits are "bad," and not all benevolent-seeming spirits have your best interests at heart. Sometimes a spirit shows up to confront you with your own shadow, or push you toward growth in uncomfortable ways. That doesn't make them evil, it just makes them part of your path. The spirit realm, like our own world, operates with complexity and purpose, not moral absolutes.

Fear is one of the biggest blocks in spirit work. And often, that fear is learned. We're taught to be afraid of certain energies before we've even encountered them. Spirits tied to death, shadow, or the underworld are often viewed with suspicion, even though they may offer powerful healing or guidance. The media has done a particularly good job of turning these archetypes into horror stories, which only furthers misinformation and anxiety around spirit contact.

Similarly, we need to stop assuming that "light" spirits – like angels or guardians – are always soft, gentle, or easy to work with. Archangels, for example, are intense. They work on a scale that can be overwhelming to human nervous systems. Their energy can be fierce, commanding, and at times deeply uncomfortable; this is not because they mean harm, but because their presence cuts through illusion and demands transformation.

Approaching spirits with intention is what makes the difference. When you work from a grounded, clear state of mind and know what you're asking for, you're far less likely to feel disoriented or outmatched. That's what balancing intentions means. You're not labeling spirits either good or bad, but understanding your own role in the interaction and owning your part of the exchange.

So much of spirit work is shaped by personal resonance: what you're naturally drawn to, what you're repelled by, and what feels energetically aligned. But it's also shaped by subconscious programming. This is why it's so important to regularly examine your own biases. Ask yourself: *Where did I learn this? Who taught me to be afraid of that? Is this fear mine, or does it belong to someone else?* This kind of self-inquiry helps dismantle the invisible narratives that can otherwise keep you disconnected from powerful, helpful spirits just because they don't "look the part."

The same goes for spirits you've been told to avoid. In truth, some of the most potent guides show up in unexpected forms: shadowy impressions, primal sensations, or dreams that stir discomfort. These spirits aren't necessarily malicious. In fact, they often act as messengers of deeper truth. They invite us to grow, stretch, and confront pieces of ourselves that we've hidden away. Spirit work, when done with clarity and intention, allows room for all of this. Not just the comfortable parts.

We also have to consider the influence of doctrine and dogma. Religious frameworks, while rich in symbolic and mythological meaning, can sometimes be restrictive when it comes to spirit contact. Some belief systems teach that only specific types of spirits are "safe," while others should be rejected outright. But spirit work doesn't respect those boundaries. Spirits don't exist within one belief system. They aren't confined to one cultural narrative. They interact with us based on energy, alignment, need, and permission.

This is the danger of gatekeeping. Within the spiritual community, it's common to encounter voices that say you must do things this way or that way, or you're doing it wrong. But spirit work isn't a closed system, it's a living, breathing, evolving relationship. It's intuitive. It's experiential. Yes, we honor tradition and learn from it, but we also give ourselves permission to be guided by direct experience, especially when that experience is respectful and rooted in integrity.

Also remember that power doesn't equal danger. A spirit can be incredibly powerful without being threatening. Many of the spirits that appear intense or overwhelming are simply carrying high frequencies, and it's our own nervous system that interprets it as a threat. The more you work with different energies, the more you learn to regulate your own system and stay centered, even in the presence of something big.

EXERCISE: A meditation for clarifying intention

The clearer your intention is, the more precise and productive your spirit work becomes. Unclear or conflicted intentions create static, like trying to tune in to a radio station with too much interference. This meditation is designed to center your energy, clear out distractions, and bring your true intentions into sharp focus.

1. **Find a quiet space where you won't be disturbed.** Sit comfortably with your spine upright. You may choose to light a candle, burn incense, or use a grounding oil, anything that helps anchor you in the moment.
2. **Close your eyes.** Inhale deeply through your nose, allowing your belly to expand. Exhale slowly through your mouth. Repeat this breath cycle three more times, letting your awareness drop from your mind into your body.
3. **Visualize a soft light forming in the center of your chest.** This is the place of your intention. With each breath, see that light growing warmer, steadier, clearer. Let it pulse gently with your breath.
4. **Now ask yourself:** *What is it that I truly seek in my spirit work?* Don't rush the answer. Let it arise. Not what you think you "should" say, but what feels true in your gut. Maybe it's clarity, healing, deeper connection, knowledge, empowerment, or service. Whatever comes up, hold it with curiosity and without judgment.
5. **Once your intention becomes clear,** imagine it forming into a symbol or word that floats in front of you in your mind's eye. This is your intention given form. Breathe into it. Feel it expand with each inhalation. As you exhale, imagine this symbol radiating out into your energy field, infusing your aura with purpose and focus.
6. **Gently bring your awareness back.** Open your eyes.

7. **You may wish to write down what came through:** your intention, the symbol, or the sensation. Revisit it often. Let it guide your actions and set the tone for every spiritual interaction moving forward.

At its core, balancing intention is about being rooted in truth. Your truth. Your practice shouldn't look like anyone else's. Spirit work isn't about replicating someone else's path; it's about uncovering your own. When you approach the work with humility, curiosity, and a willingness to be transformed, the spirits meet you there.

You don't have to be perfect. You don't need to have all the answers. You just need to keep showing up with clear intention, grounded energy, and an open heart. The rest will unfold exactly as it needs to.

PRACTICE SUMMARY

- Before beginning any ritual, write down your intention in one clear sentence.
- Ask yourself: *Does this serve growth, healing, or wisdom?* If not, revise it.
- Practice balancing your intention by pairing it with gratitude; for example, when asking also give thanks.
- Finally, burn or bury a written intention.

CHAPTER 5

Working with spirit allies

Spirits are not so different from people; they are diverse, layered, often unpredictable, and capable of holding many truths at once. Just as no two humans walk the exact same path, no two spirits express themselves in exactly the same way. Trying to force these beings into neat little categories or moral labels is not only misguided, but it limits our capacity to understand the complexity and power they offer. Spirit work isn't about placing spirits into tidy boxes labeled "good" or "bad." It's about relationship. It's about resonance. It's about listening.

That said, over time and through experience, certain types of spirits tend to show up again and again. They carry distinct energies, purposes, and patterns in how they interact with the living. In this chapter are some of the common spirit presences you might encounter on this path; a set of familiar landmarks rather than a complete map. As always, if something doesn't resonate with your experience, trust that. Use what aligns. Leave the rest.

Ancestors and beloved dead

Some of the most accessible spirits for many practitioners are our ancestors and beloved dead. These spirits usually have a direct tie to us, either through bloodline, chosen family, or soul connection. Because of that bond, they tend to be more invested in our well-being and more responsive to our outreach.

When we talk about "ancestors," we don't just mean biological relatives. Ancestors can include cultural ancestors, spiritual lineage bearers, and anyone whose life and legacy paved the way for yours. Honoring them isn't romanticizing the past, but recognizing that we are not here by accident. We are here because of those who came before.

Establishing a relationship with these spirits often begins with simple acts of remembrance. Set up a small altar with photos, heirlooms, or offerings that feel significant: coffee, bread, flowers, handwritten notes. Light a candle. Speak their names. Invite their presence. Let it feel real. You might say:

> *"I honor those whose blood and spirit*
> *run through me. I remember you.*
> *I welcome you. I'm listening."*

Trust that showing up consistently builds the relationship. These spirits may communicate through dreams, gut instincts, or sudden flashes of insight. You might feel a particular warmth, scent, or presence when they draw near. Working with ancestors can be a source of strength, healing, and protection but it can also bring up inherited wounds. That's part of the process. Spirit work isn't always light and love; it's truth. And sometimes truth asks us to sit with what's been passed down so we can choose what we carry forward and what we lay to rest.

ANCESTOR RITUAL

Call upon spirits of the dead, especially ancestors, when you need guidance rooted in legacy, family healing, and personal identity. These spirits often respond well to offerings that connect to their lives or culture: a cup of coffee, a favorite scent, the sound of their language or music. Attune to them by spending time in reflection, visiting their gravesites if accessible, or building an altar space with photos and items that honor their memory.

Affirmation to open communication:

"I honor those who came before me,
whose lives made mine possible. If you
walk with love and good intention,
you are welcome in this space."

RITUAL TIP: Light a white candle and place a small cup of water before it. Speak aloud the ancestors' names (if known) or simply invite "those of my blood and spirit who walk in peace." Sit in silence and allow their presence to speak to you through sensation or inner knowing.

Nature allies and land spirits

Nature spirits are vast, diverse, and incredibly present. From the spirit of a specific tree or mountain to the consciousness within rivers, wind, and stone, these are the spirits of the land and the natural world. They hold ancient memory. They move with the seasons and tides. These spirits don't use human language, but they are always communicating, through sensation, cycles, and intuitive nudges. Connecting with nature spirits begins with reverence. Go outside with presence. Leave offerings. Touch the earth. Listen more than you speak.

If you live in an urban area, know that these spirits are still there. The spirit of the land exists beneath the concrete. The wind moves through alleyways just like it does through forest trails. Find your rhythm with them.

CONNECTING WITH LAND SPIRITS

Connect with land spirits when you're doing grounding work, seeking creative flow, or needing clarity about your purpose. Their energy is deeply tied to place, so build relationships slowly. Introduce yourself before asking for anything. Leave small gifts: flowers, water, song, or biodegradable offerings. These spirits can guide your path when you're attuned to their rhythms. Spend time quietly in nature. Observe without speaking for several minutes, grounding your energy through your breath. Place your hand on the earth and silently offer a blessing. Listen. Feel.

When seeking connection, you might say:

"I honor the spirit of this land. I walk with respect. If you're open to connection, I'm listening and ready to learn."

Build the relationship slowly, as you would with any sentient being. You may be called to leave offerings like seeds, spring water, or even song. Don't force connection; nature spirits often reveal themselves in their own time.

Celestial and cosmic beings

Celestial spirits encompass beings sometimes called angels, archangels, or other radiant intelligences associated with what many would consider divine or cosmic realms. While pop culture and religious imagery may portray these beings as purely benevolent, light-filled protectors, the reality (at least in my experience) is more layered.

Celestial spirits aren't here to coddle us. These powerful forces often move with clarity and precision, not sentimentality. They don't operate on human timelines or emotional frameworks. If you call on a celestial being, especially one of the higher order, be prepared for the energy to feel intense, even overwhelming at first. It's not harmful, but it shifts everything. Think of it like standing in sunlight after being in a cave for hours. The light is beautiful, yes, but it can also be disorienting.

Working with celestial spirits can be deeply rewarding when you approach them with respect and a clear heart. These spirits are especially helpful for higher guidance, healing, spiritual clarity, or when you're seeking strength during a period of transformation. You might invoke them in times of spiritual crisis or when you feel a call to realign with your purpose.

Approach them through prayer, meditation, or sacred space. Speak your truth clearly. Use affirming language: "I open to clarity and guidance," or "I welcome alignment and truth." You may feel their presence as a warmth, pressure on the chest, sudden peace, or ringing in the ears. Often, these spirits don't speak in words but in waves of knowing.

Just remember, these spirits are not religious property. They don't belong to one tradition or dogma. While their names and forms may appear across many belief systems, what matters is your relationship with them. Don't be afraid to find your own way into connection.

COMMUNICATING WITH CELESTIAL SPIRITS

Call upon celestial spirits when your focus is on expansion, soul memory, or accessing a broader perspective. These beings may communicate through dreams, meditations, and subtle energetic downloads. They tend to come through when you're open and quiet, rather than when you're chasing them. Attune to them through stargazing, working with planetary hours, or inviting connection during sleep.

Try this invocation:

"I open my heart to the wisdom of the cosmos. May those of the stars who walk in truth guide me gently to remembrance."

Sit beneath the night sky or in a darkened room with a lit candle. Visualize starlight filling your body, soft and intelligent. Speak a question or intention aloud and remain still. Let answers arrive however they come.

Deities and divine spirits

Deities are distinct spiritual presences, divine intelligences that may be shaped by culture, myth, and mystery. Some feel vast and cosmic, while others are immediate and personal. They are not abstract archetypes but real, conscious beings who can choose to walk with you, teach you, challenge you, or bless your life.

These spirits may reach out through dreams, symbols, synchronicities, or strong pulls toward a name or image. Other times, the connection is initiated through prayer or curiosity. Either way, the foundation is respect. This isn't blind devotion, but building relationship with clear intention and sincere humility.

Work with deities when you want to deepen your spiritual path, embody a certain quality or archetype, or receive guidance that speaks to the soul's larger journey. These spirits may help you step into sovereignty, protection, purpose, healing, or sacred rebellion.

WORKING WITH DEITIES

If you feel drawn to a deity, start by learning about their origins. Read myths. Listen for their symbols in your life. When you feel ready, introduce yourself, either in meditation, with a letter, or at an altar. Don't ask for anything at first. Just offer your presence and see if the energy responds.

Begin the relationship slowly, with reverence. You might say:

"If it is your will, [Name], I ask to walk with you. Show me how I may honor your presence and receive your guidance."

Offerings may include incense, candlelight, flowers, specific foods, poetry, or time spent in their honor. What matters most is your sincerity behind the gesture.

Some deities are fierce. Others are subtle. They may challenge you as much as they bless you. Make space for the relationship to evolve. Keep your intentions clear. And if something ever feels out of alignment, you have the right to pause, reassess, and re-ground. Let the connection unfold in its own rhythm, trusting that you will be guided to what is meant for you. This is a sacred relationship, not a spiritual transaction.

Practice tip: When beginning a relationship with a new deity, write a letter to them first. Express what you're seeking, and what you're offering in return: devotion, time, integrity, alignment. Burn or bury the letter as a gesture of surrender and trust.

Challenging spirits, shadow beings, or trickster spirits

These spirits are some of the most misunderstood and, frankly, avoided beings in spirit work. That's understandable. They challenge order, disrupt plans, and push you into uncomfortable truths. But that doesn't make them bad; sometimes it makes them necessary.

The trickster archetype exists in nearly every spiritual tradition: Loki, Hermes, Coyote, Eshu, Raven. These spirits may bring transformation through disruption. They teach by flipping the script, sometimes with humor, other times with chaos. If you're too rigid in your thinking or clinging to illusions, a trickster might show up to knock things loose.

Working with these spirits isn't for everyone, and it's not always easy. But when you approach them with humility and respect, they can be powerful allies for growth, especially when you've hit a spiritual plateau. They challenge the ego. They invite creativity. They force you to see what you'd rather ignore.

APPROACHING TRICKSTER SPIRITS

If you choose to work with a trickster spirit, be very clear about your intentions. State your boundaries. Be honest with yourself about what you're asking for, and be ready for the answer to come in unexpected ways. You might light a candle and say:

"If you have a lesson for me, I'm open, but teach gently."

Then listen. Watch. Pay attention to synchronicities and unexpected twists.

While they don't always play nice, they don't play aimlessly either. When facing spirits that provoke fear, confusion, or discomfort, it's important to remain grounded and neutral. Not all challenging spirits are harmful; some are simply misunderstood or mirror parts of ourselves we haven't accepted yet. Still, discernment is key. Use protection rituals and shielding practices, and do not attempt to work with these spirits unless you feel stable and supported.

Grounding words:

"I see you, spirit, and acknowledge your presence. If you walk in truth and balance, you may remain. If not, I release you with peace."

Safety practice tip: Use a black candle, protective herbs (like rosemary or rue), and a bowl of salted water. Speaking aloud, set clear boundaries before beginning any communication. If energy feels sharp, draining, or overwhelming, end the session and cleanse yourself and your space immediately.

EXERCISE: Attunement ritual for spirit connection

Before initiating any form of spirit communication, I recommend creating a grounded, intentional space. Start by cleansing your environment in whatever way feels aligned for you. This could be with smoke, sound, or even visualization. Then light a candle to symbolize your intention and bring a sense of focus to the space.

Take a moment to ground yourself. Close your eyes, breathe deeply, and feel the weight of your body anchoring into the earth. Allow any distractions or residual energy from the day to fall away. You want to enter this space with clarity and presence.

When you're ready, speak your intention aloud. Something simple is usually best:

> ***"I open this space in clarity and respect. I invite connection with the spirit of [name or type of spirit]. May this be a safe, mutual, and clear exchange."***

Make an offering. This doesn't have to be elaborate; spirits often respond more to sincerity than extravagance. You might offer a small glass of water, a few words of appreciation, a candle flame, or your full attention. The point is to give, not just ask.

Now, allow yourself to receive. Sit in stillness. Don't force anything. Pay attention to what shifts emotionally, energetically, even physically. Sometimes it's a sensation in the room, a change in temperature, or a subtle feeling of presence. Other times there's nothing, and that's okay. Spirit communication builds over time.

When the moment feels complete, close the space. Express gratitude, either silently or aloud:

> *"Thank you for your presence. I honor this connection. I release the space in peace."*

Blow out the candle. Pour out the water offering. Touch something physical to reconnect to the present moment. Then take a few minutes to write down what you experienced. Over time, these small notes can become a powerful archive of your spiritual development and the relationships you're forming.

No matter what kind of spirit you're working with, the foundation is the same: respect, intention, and self-awareness. You don't need to know everything. You just need to work with integrity. And as you grow in your practice, you'll learn how each spirit teaches, responds, and moves with you. Spirit work isn't about domination or control. It's not about collecting contacts in the unseen realms like spiritual Pokémon. It's a relationship. And like all relationships, it takes time, presence, and reciprocity.

PRACTICE SUMMARY

» Spend time outdoors and acknowledge the land, trees, or elements present. Speak a simple greeting aloud.

» Create a respectful offering practice (such as fresh water, incense, or a song).

» When you sense a presence, quietly ask its role or purpose. Write down what impressions come.

» Keep notes on recurring spirits or energies; notice patterns in how they appear to you.

CHAPTER 6

Preparing your space and practice

Having a sacred space is the foundation for meaningful spirit work. In this chapter, we focus on creating and maintaining that space while also exploring the principles that support a strong and respectful practice. You'll learn about the etiquette, awareness, and reciprocal relationships that help you build a solid foundation for connecting with spirits. By understanding these ideas and putting them into practice when creating your space, you will set the stage for interactions that are grounded, positive, and deeply rewarding.

Research first

Research is critical in spirit work. To create a relationship with a spirit, you must first fully comprehend them. When you discover more about a spirit, research will help you strengthen your bond with them, which is essential if you wish to work together. Because the etiquette for engaging with different spirits varies, you must recognize who or what you're dealing with. Deities, for example, have distinct requirements for devotees, and those standards may vary with each pantheon. If you choose to connect with your ancestors, how you communicate and act with them depends on who they were in life: their character, culture, and beliefs. This is why it's important to know beforehand who it is you are connecting with.

Learning who you're connecting with is simple, especially with deities. Most who venture into spirit work feel compelled to research what interests them or what attracts them, like a particular pantheon, or a certain god or goddess. With the plethora of information now available, it's easy to research their history and myths.

Lesser-known spirits like land spirits and spirits of place can be more challenging to find information on, but there are some things you can do to help. For instance, acknowledge the kind of spirit you are interacting with: ancestral spirit, land spirit, and so on. Next, look for examples of what a particular spirit is usually like and how they are characterized. Lastly, consider how your discoveries apply to the spirit you want to interact with.

If you want to connect with your home spirits, for example, a good place to start is looking at how different cultures engage and connect with them. You may notice that people occasionally make food or drink offerings. Discovering more about your local environment's flora and wildlife can also help in learning more about a spirit. Did the spirit live in a tree before coming to you? What were their origins and what shape would they take?

Would it be small, nimble, and humanoid, or would it resemble a typical house spider? Finding answers to these questions can help you have a better idea of how to go forward and develop a bond with spirits.

Be considerate

Being respectful of spirits means more than just being polite. Although proper etiquette is important when interacting and forming a relationship with a spirit, the way in which you display that etiquette is largely based on who you are interacting with. Good manners differ depending on culture and history, and what being polite means with one spirit may be different with another. Not every spirit wants a lengthy or thorough ritual with tools and chants, but keep in mind that any interactions with them should be met with thoughtfulness and appropriate consideration. Even when banishing a spirit, respect goes a long way. These are powerful entities and need to be treated as such. Good manners will have an effect on your desired results and help you to avoid any negative consequences.

Generally, good manners include things like being civil and leaving offerings. Once your interaction is complete, expressing gratitude is also polite; however, be attentive to who the spirit is, because according to fairy lore, saying thank you is a no-no. You can express your gratitude in better ways. There are many reasons why a spirit will not connect with you, or you will not want to work with a spirit. Don't try to push it. It's important to be courteous to maintain good standing. Look at it as an opportunity: whether a spirit dismisses you or you refuse to work with them, the spirit doesn't want to waste your time, and you shouldn't feel forced to create a connection. If you feel obliged to leave an offering, respect their intentions, or respectfully decline with your reasons, express your appreciation clearly and confidently, and move on.

Reciprocate

Like any successful human relationship, a spiritual partnership needs a balance of give and take. You need a mutually beneficial relationship to properly interact with spirits; a spiritual ally is not supposed to be a one-sided service. Spirits won't simply perform what you request without expecting anything in return. Similarly, if you put in the effort to develop a relationship and honor it, you will be rewarded.

Offerings should not be considered as payment for what you want; it's more complicated than that. The importance of offerings is that they grant more power to a spirit, and preferred or better offerings can persuade a spirit's willingness to assist you or build a stronger relationship with you. Generally, you should make an offering upon meeting a spirit as a polite introduction. Before asking for anything in return, it's also traditional to make an offering. Offerings, however, should not be made just for the purpose of receiving something in return. Imagine if a friend attempted to obligate you into performing favors by demanding something in return every time they did something for you. You may begin to doubt their motives and feel used, knowing that their goal is to obtain something from you. To avoid this type of agenda, make offerings regularly. Offerings may not necessarily be substantial or tangible. A prayer, poem, or loving energy can all be offerings if you intend them to be. Be creative and think about or research what kind of things your spirit ally would like. Consider when a friend's birthday is approaching, you may purchase a present or bake a cake for them. The same can be said about spirits: some enjoy complex and expensive items, while others appreciate the thought and care that goes into gifts. By taking the time to know them, you can figure out what kinds of gifts they enjoy and what they're capable of providing in return. You wouldn't necessarily petition a war goddess for a more loving partner, for instance. Specificity is important.

Partner

Spirits should be treated with mutual kindness and respect. Much like in a human relationship, a healthy spiritual partnership requires time, care, and effort. Spirit work takes time and dedication, so if that sounds like too much work for you, keep in mind that not everyone is required to participate in the work. It's fine if you accept that it will take a lot more energy and time than you'd like to devote to your practice. If you'd prefer to wait because of the needed commitment, it doesn't mean you're not capable of manifesting on your own.

EXERCISE: Creating a sacred space

Creating a sacred space for spirit work is more than the physical surroundings; it is a deliberate act of spiritual preparation and alignment. Begin by selecting a quiet area or room where you feel comfortable and undisturbed. Sit or stand in the center of this space, taking a moment to close your eyes and consciously shift your focus inward.

1. **Take several deep breaths.** Allow each inhalation to fill you with calmness and each exhalation to release any tension or distractions. As you breathe, visualize a sphere of radiant light forming around you, extending from the ground beneath your feet to the ceiling above your head. This sphere is a boundary of protection and sacredness, shimmering with a color that resonates with you, perhaps a soothing white or a grounding earthy tone.
2. **Feel this sphere anchoring you firmly to the earth.** It's connecting you deeply with its stable energy. At the same time, imagine it reaching upward, touching the heavens and drawing down divine light and guidance. This connection serves as a channel for spiritual energies to flow freely and harmoniously within your space.
3. **Invite spirit to join you.** You may choose to call upon spiritual beings or entities you work with and trust – such as guides, guardians, or ancestors – to join you in this sacred endeavor. Invite them with respect and openness, asking for their protection, wisdom, and support as you engage in spirit work.
4. **Use tools to enhance your space's ambiance and energetics.** Consider using tools such as incense, candles, crystals, or sacred objects that hold personal significance. These items can serve as focal points for concentration and intention, amplifying the spiritual energies present and reinforcing the sanctity of your space.

5. **Consecrate the space.** As you continue to breathe deeply and consciously, affirm silently or aloud that this space is now consecrated and prepared for spirit work. Declare that only energies of love, light, and positivity are welcome within this sphere, and that any lower vibrations or negativity stay respectfully outside of its boundaries.

6. **Observe what you have created.** When you feel fully centered and aligned within your sacred space, gradually open your eyes and take a moment to observe the tranquil environment you have cultivated. Notice how the atmosphere feels lighter, clearer, and imbued with a sense of reverence and readiness for spiritual exploration.

Remember, maintaining a sacred space is an ongoing practice that requires regular attention and intention. Take time before each session of spirit work to reinforce its sanctity and ensure that your space remains a potent haven for your spiritual practice. By nurturing and respecting your sacred space, you create a supportive foundation for deepening your connection with the spiritual realms and accessing profound insights and guidance.

A LAYERED SPACE

When preparing a space for spirit work, I find it useful to think in terms of layers: physical, energetic, and intentional. First, address the physical layer by tidying, dusting, or cleansing the space with smoke, salt, or sound. Second, attend to the energetic layer through prayer, visualization, or creating a circle. The final layer is intention. You can shift the atmosphere simply by lighting a candle while saying: "This space is protected, open, and ready for clear connection."

Try this for yourself. Journal what it feels like before and what's different after. Over time, these small rituals build a rhythm that tells both your spirit allies and your own subconscious that you are stepping into sacred work.

PRACTICE SUMMARY

- Choose a space that feels calm and designate it for your spiritual work.
- Cleanse it physically (tidy, dust, remove clutter) before energetic cleansing.
- Try one method of energetic clearing: smoke, sound, or salt. Notice which feels most effective for you.
- Build a simple altar with one or two objects that symbolize grounding and connection.

CHAPTER 7

Anchoring your energy

When working with spirits, energies, or any subtle realms, one of the most important foundations you can have is a reliable way to anchor your energy. Too often, people rush into spirit communication or magical work without first learning how to protect and stabilize their own energy, then they wonder why they feel drained, anxious, or overwhelmed. These practices are essential, not optional. By the end of this chapter, you'll know how to make them a natural part of your practice, transforming the way you connect with the subtle realms.

Grounding

This is the act of anchoring your energy into the earth. It brings you back into your body, into presence, and helps you release excess or scattered energy. Spirit work requires that you be both open and rooted, attuned to higher frequencies while also being firmly connected to the physical plane. Think of it like electricity: without grounding, the energy has nowhere to go safely.

There are many ways to ground. One of the simplest is to stand barefoot on the earth, grass, dirt, or sand and consciously release energy through the soles of your feet.

Visualize roots extending from your body deep into the earth, drawing stability, nourishment, and clarity up into you.

You can also ground through movement, food, breath, or visualization. Sitting quietly with your hands on your thighs and slowly breathing into your belly while imagining yourself solid and steady like a mountain can work wonders. What matters is intention. You're calling your energy back to yourself and anchoring it in the present.

You should ground before and after all spirit work, when you feel overwhelmed or scattered, and when your intuition is cloudy or your emotions are intense. It's not just a safety tool; it's a returning to yourself.

Shielding

This is your energetic boundary. Shielding is what keeps unwanted influences out of your space, whether that's the emotions of others, residual spiritual energy, or even entities you haven't invited in.

Shielding doesn't mean shutting yourself off or living in fear. It means being discerning about what you allow in your field. It's about sovereignty. You get to decide what enters and what doesn't. A good shield isn't rigid or impenetrable, but flexible, responsive, and empowering.

There are many ways to shield. The most common is visual: close your eyes and imagine a field of energy surrounding your body. This could look like a shimmering bubble, a cloak of light, a mirrored surface, or even armor made of natural elements. The imagery doesn't matter as much as the feeling. Your shield should feel strong, secure, and personal to you.

Set the intention. You can speak these aloud or repeat them internally while visualizing your shield activating:

> *"Only energies aligned with my highest good may enter this space."*
>
> *Or "I am protected, grounded, and sovereign in my energy."*

You might reinforce your shield by anointing your body with protective oils (such as rosemary, frankincense, or cedar), wearing specific crystals (such as black tourmaline or obsidian), or carrying charm bags with protective herbs. Physical tools help, but your belief and intention are what energize the shield.

Shielding should become a regular part of your spiritual hygiene. Do it when entering crowded places, before doing any spiritual work, and after engaging with others who feel energetically draining. Shielding takes just a few moments, but it can make all the difference in how you feel and how clearly you can tune into spirit.

THE MIRROR BUBBLE

A simple shielding practice is what I call the "mirror bubble." Visualize yourself surrounded by a sphere of light that reflects back anything that isn't yours to carry. See it as clear, strong, and bright. This is not about pushing energy away with force, but setting a natural boundary. If you prefer something more tangible, carry a small stone like black tourmaline or hematite in your pocket and set the intention that it holds your shield throughout the day. Shields don't need to be complicated; they just need to feel real to you.

Centering

Centering brings your awareness back to you. It's the practice of calling your energy home, reclaiming your focus, presence, and power. When you're centered, you're not scattered or pulled in a thousand directions. You're in alignment with your core.

Centering is especially useful after emotional overwhelm, spiritual work, or any experience where your energy feels "off." It's also essential to center before any kind of ritual, spirit communication, or divination. Without centering, it's easy to mistake external noise for intuition or get lost in someone else's energy.

To center, close your eyes and take a few slow, deep breaths. Place your hand on your solar plexus or heart, somewhere you can anchor your awareness. Visualize your energy gathering to the center of your being. You might imagine threads of light returning to your core from wherever they've been stretched or pulled. With each breath, affirm:

> *"I call my energy back to me.*
> *I am here. I am whole."*

Sometimes it helps to speak your name aloud or gently tap your chest. This creates a somatic cue to help bring your energy into alignment. You might also visualize a flame at the center of your chest, steady and unwavering – your inner compass, your spiritual center.

EXERCISE: Center, ground, and shield

1. **Find a quiet, comfortable space.** One where you won't be interrupted. Sit in a way that feels natural; on the floor, in a chair, or with your back supported. Gently close your eyes and begin to slow your breath. Inhale through the nose, hold for a moment, then exhale through the mouth.
2. **Start to count.** Inhale for one. Hold. Exhale for one. Inhale for two, hold, and exhale for two. Then inhale for three … and so on, up to five. With each count, let your thoughts fall away. Don't fight them, just let them pass like clouds. If your mind wanders, start back at one. There's no rush.
3. **Visualize your heart.** When you reach the count of five and your breath is steady, bring your awareness to your heart space. Visualize a glowing sphere of light beginning to form there. This is your center, your energy. See it pulsing, growing, swirling outward. Let this energy expand until it gently envelops your entire body. You may feel warmth, tingling, or a sense of peace. Trust whatever arises.

4. **Send this light downward into the ground beneath you.** Feel it anchoring you to the earth. Feel your roots go deep. Then send that same energy upward, toward the sky, the stars, the cosmos. Imagine yourself lit from within, connected to above and below, grounded and radiant.

5. **Allow that energy to form a soft, protective shield around you.** It's like a second skin or a bubble of golden light. You can speak your intention aloud:

   "Only energy aligned with my highest good may enter this space."

6. **Stay here for a few more breaths.** Feel the stillness. Let your guides draw close if they wish. You are safe. You are centered. You are seen. This is the place from which spirit work begins.

When you are centered, grounded, and shielded, you become a clear vessel. You can sense spiritual energies more accurately, discern what's yours and what isn't, and engage with spirits from a place of authority and peace. These three practices work together to support your sovereignty and safety. They form the foundation of all spirit work. When you are anchored in yourself, you cannot be easily swayed by fear, distraction, or external influence.

These are not one-time practices. They're rituals of return. Incorporate them daily or as needed until they become second nature. You'll notice the difference, not just in your spirit work, but in how you move through the world.

PRACTICE SUMMARY

- » Practice daily grounding by visualizing roots from your body into the earth.
- » Experiment with a personal shield: imagine a bubble or a cloak of light. See which feels strongest.
- » Center by placing one hand over your heart and breathing slowly until your energy steadies.
- » Note how each technique changes your sense of presence before and after spirit work.

CHAPTER 8

Protection magic

Before any protective tool or ritual can be truly effective, your intent must be clear. Intent is the energetic blueprint of your magic, what shapes and directs the forces you're calling in. Without it, even the most time-tested ritual may feel hollow or ineffective.

Intent doesn't have to be poetic or elaborate. Simplicity often makes it stronger. The statements: "I am safe," "My energy is my own," or "I release what does not serve me" can be just as potent as complex invocations. What matters is that it's true to your purpose, felt in your body, and spoken (or thought) with presence. Setting intent is an energetic act of claiming space. Before a ritual, spell, or energetic practice, breathe and ground into your body. Ask yourself: *Why am I doing this? What outcome do I seek?* From there, let your intention rise naturally.

WHY DO PROTECTION MAGIC?

Protection magic isn't about fear, it's about sovereignty. It's about knowing that your energy, space, and spirit are sacred, and honoring them accordingly. Protection practices help you maintain clarity, vitality, and alignment, especially when engaging in spirit work.

Before you engage in any protection work – whether you're dressing a door with oil, placing stones around your space, or calling in your guardians – your intention should already be clear. Speak it out loud if the space allows, or whisper it if you must. Think your intention firmly if that's what the moment requires. However you express it, it should be present, grounded, and aligned with what you are asking for.

EXERCISE: A ritual for anchoring intent

1. **Start by grounding.** Take some slow, steady breaths. Feel your feet flat on the floor. Imagine roots extending downward, anchoring you to the earth below. Then center yourself. Bring your attention inward, toward your solar plexus, your heart, or wherever you feel your power lives. This is where your energy pools.
2. **Speak your intention.** You can say it silently or aloud:

   "I protect this space. I call all of my energy home. I fortify my boundaries. I am safe."

3. **Seal the work.** To mark the shift, you might clap once, ring a bell, anoint yourself with oil, or simply release a steady breath. Let your body register that something has begun.

There's no single "right" way to protect yourself spiritually. What matters most is what feels aligned, grounded, and effective for you. The following techniques are tools, not rules. They're meant to be customized and adapted to your practice, your energy, and your spirits.

Some protections are subtle, woven into daily routines. Others are more involved, used when you're doing deeper spirit work or feeling energetically exposed. Use what you need, when you need it.

Rituals for protection

Salt and boundary work

Salt has been used as a purifier and protector across many traditions. It creates a boundary that's energetically clear and difficult for unwanted energies to cross. Sprinkle a thin line of salt across thresholds – doorways and windowsills – and the perimeter of your home. If you live in an apartment or can't sprinkle salt openly, a small bowl of salt placed near the front door works just as well.

Use this technique when you're feeling vulnerable to external energy, or after spirit contact has left your space feeling murky. It's also helpful during spiritual cleansings or after conflict in the home.

Smoke cleansing

Smoke has long been used to carry prayers, cleanse spaces, and shift energy. Whether you use herbal bundles, incense, or resins, what matters is your intention and respect for the plant spirits. Because white sage is often commercialized and overharvested, you can turn to local herbs or ethically sourced blends. Suggested options: rosemary, cedar, lavender, mugwort, frankincense.

Always thank the plant spirit and work with it intentionally. Use smoke cleansing when you've had visitors in your space; after ritual work; or when you feel heavy, stuck, or energetically cluttered.

Protective oils and anointing

Oils can be used to anoint candles, doors, tools, or your own body. You can purchase a protection oil or create your own using a carrier oil (such as olive or jojoba oil) and protective herbs such as basil, rosemary, bay, or cinnamon. Add a few drops of essential oil, if desired, and always consecrate the oil with purpose.

To anoint, dab a small amount on your pulse points, over your heart, or on the soles of your feet before a ritual. Trace protective symbols on doors, mirrors, or tools. Use this technique when you're doing deep spirit work, heading into public spaces where energy feels dense, or reinforcing your home's energetic boundaries.

Crystals and stones

Certain stones naturally offer shielding properties. Black tourmaline, obsidian, hematite, onyx, smoky quartz, and labradorite are a few of the most commonly used. Cleanse and charge them regularly. Wear, carry, or place them in your space.

This technique is for when you want to maintain energetic sovereignty throughout the day, especially if you're highly sensitive or frequently in crowded spaces. Stones also work well for reinforcing spiritual boundaries during spirit communication.

Spiritual baths

More than just relaxation rituals, spiritual baths cleanse the auric field, clear spiritual residue, and reinforce protection. You can create a bath with salt (Epsom or sea), protective herbs, essential oils, and even spoken affirmations. Soak in silence or with soft music. Let the water carry away what doesn't belong.

You can use this technique when you've finished a spirit session, feel spiritually "off," or are preparing for important work. Sometimes what keeps you safe isn't what's visible, but what's encoded with meaning. Protection can be layered in symbols you wear, draw, or carry. These elements work like energetic signatures, holding intention and presence even when you're focused elsewhere.

Protective symbols

Across spiritual traditions, symbols have long been used to hold protective power. The key is choosing what resonates with your lineage, practice, or personal resonance. Some common examples include:

- The eye (in various forms like the evil eye or eye of Horus) to deflect harm
- The pentacle for protection and balance
- The crossroads symbol for spiritual gateways and warding
- Spirals or circles as wards of wholeness and containment

Draw these symbols on your front door, on your mirror, or in your journal. Etch them on candles or wear them as jewelry. Speak to them. Activate them with breath and belief. Feel free to use this technique when you're entering spirit communication, traveling, or moving through vulnerable transitions.

Sigils

These are charged symbols created from intention. You take a phrase (such as "I am safe and protected"), distill it into letters, and then into a symbolic design. This is your private language with spirit. The act of creating the sigil becomes the first layer of protection; empowering it is the second.

Charge a sigil through meditation, visualization, burning, or placing it under moonlight. Then draw it where it's needed: on the soles of your shoes, inside your wallet, on the inside of a charm bag, or on a candle. If you'd like, use this technique when you want custom protection that's unique to your energy and your intent.

Charm bags and carried protection

Charm bags are old magic. They're physical anchors for spiritual intention: bundles of herbs, stones, written words, and symbols. You can carry them on your person, place under your pillow, hang near your front door, or bury at the threshold of your home.

To create a protective charm bag, choose a small pouch. Black, red, or white are common for protection, but go with what feels right.

Add the following:

- Pinch of salt or black pepper for warding
- Dried protective herbs such as rosemary, bay leaf, or angelica root
- Crystal or stone such as black tourmaline or obsidian
- Written affirmation or sigil for protection
- Optional: a garlic clove (dried), nail (for piercing or anchoring energy), or charm that holds personal meaning

Before sealing the bag, breathe your intention into it. Speak directly to the contents:

> *"Guard me. Protect my path.*
> *Shield my energy."*

Tie the pouch shut, wear it close, and recharge it regularly either under moonlight, with smoke, or through breath and voice. Charm bags are great to use when you're working with spirits, traveling, going into unfamiliar territory, or simply when your energy feels exposed.

* * *

Protection isn't a one-time spell or charm, but a living practice. Just like you lock your doors each night or wash your hands after being out in public, energetic protection needs tending. Especially if you're doing regular spirit work or moving through high-sensitivity days. Your spiritual hygiene should feel intuitive, not burdensome. The more you do it, the more naturally it integrates into your rhythm.

EXERCISE: Assessing your boundaries

Sometimes we only realize our protections have weakened after the fact, when we feel drained, heavy, scattered, or invaded. Check in with yourself regularly. Ask yourself:

1. Do I feel like my energy is mine?
2. Have I had unusual emotional spikes that aren't mine?

3. Do I feel open, exposed, or energetically "leaky"?
4. Have I had troubling dreams, uncharacteristic irritability, or a fog that won't lift?

These aren't always signs of spiritual interference but invitations to pause, ground, and reset. If you're deepening your practice, encountering unfamiliar entities, or experiencing an uptick in activity, your protections may need to evolve. Spirit work isn't static. Your protective practices should grow with your sensitivity, your depth, and the frequency at which you operate.

You can combine methods like using a charm bag while also anointing doorways, layering symbols on your altar, and setting wards around your home. Let your intuition lead, and always return to your root intention: safety, sovereignty, and clarity. You don't need to fear engaging with the spirit world but you do need to be mindful. Protection is about discernment, autonomy, and trust. With the right foundations in place, your spirit work can unfold with depth, safety, and empowerment.

Banishing

There are moments in spiritual work when grounding, shielding, and warding don't feel enough. Maybe something's lingering in your space. Maybe the energy just won't shift. Maybe you feel watched, drained, or like you're not alone, even when you are. This is when banishing becomes necessary. Banishing is not about fear or control, but boundaries. It's about clearing out what doesn't belong and reclaiming sovereignty.

Banishing is not always aggressive. It can be as quiet as a whispered intention or as forceful as a thunderclap of will. The energy behind it isn't punishment, but declaring, "This is not your place." It is spiritual hygiene on a large scale. You banish when there's a presence that refuses to leave, or energy that clings. You banish when your intuitive senses say, "Something's off," and your usual protections don't restore balance. You can use banishing after spirit contact when something feels sticky or unresolved. Use it when an object holds an attachment. And sometimes it's needed simply because the veil has thinned, and things are wandering through that aren't meant to stay.

Before performing any banishing, pause and assess: *Is this energy external or internal?* Sometimes what we feel as an "unwanted spirit" is actually our own projections, fears, or unresolved emotions. Banishing should never be your first move. But when it's needed, it works best when rooted in clarity, groundedness, and authority.

There are countless forms of banishing, from smoke rituals and sacred sound to ceremonial rites and planetary hours. In this section, I'll share what's worked in my own practice, including energetic and more structured approaches. You don't need to be part of a ceremonial tradition to do this work, but you do need to be firm in your presence, focused in your will, and clear about what you're asking to leave.

When done well, banishing is equal parts intention and action. You're creating a shift in energy, telling any lingering spirit or uninvited force that it's time to move on. That shift can be subtle or forceful. What matters most is that you believe in the energy behind your words and movements.

Sometimes I've used banishing after a house clearing, when the energy felt muddy or something didn't respond to softer methods. Other times I've used it after a deep session of mediumship, when a spirit hung on longer than they should have. I've also used banishing on objects – crystals, thrifted items, tools – which carried something that wasn't mine.

Smoke and sound

Smoke is one of the oldest and most intuitive tools we have. Burn dried herbs like rosemary, mugwort, or frankincense and let the smoke drift through the corners of your space. As it moves, speak aloud:

> *"This space is mine. Any energy not aligned with my highest good must leave now."*

You can get more specific if you like, but the core of the work is your voice, focus, and presence.

Sound does something similar; it breaks up energy. Clap your hands loudly in corners or ring a bell. I keep a small Tibetan bowl on my altar for this. The vibration moves through stagnant energy and shifts it, especially when paired with breath and intention.

Salt and water

Salt is grounding and cleansing. I've sprinkled salt on thresholds when a space felt psychically cluttered, then swept it out with a firm intention. You can dissolve it in water and flick it around a room, or leave small bowls in corners temporarily to absorb unwanted energy. You can also make a banishing wash; infuse water with rosemary, basil, or rue; and wipe down doors, windows, mirrors, and reflective surfaces.

Banishing through fire

Fire transforms. Write down what needs to be removed – whether it's an energy, pattern, or connection – and burn it safely. I do this when I want to be very direct, especially if something is repeating. Speak to the flame:

> *"I release this fully. This no longer has space in my field."*

Fire doesn't need to be dramatic; it can be as simple as a candle if your intent is strong and clear.

Energetic banishing with visualization

You don't always need tools. One of the strongest forms of banishing I've used involves just breath and visualization. Ground yourself deeply. Then visualize a wave of energy, your energy, sweeping through the space. I often see it as golden or electric light. Move it through every corner and say clearly:

> *"Any spirit or energy that does not belong here, leave now. You are not welcome in this space. You must go."*

Repeat this as needed. This technique has helped me release wandering spirits who may have been lost, stuck, or simply curious.

Working with allies

At times, you'll want to call on spiritual allies, guides, ancestors, guardians, or even deities known for boundary-setting (such as Hekate, Archangel Michael, or traditional warding spirits). Let them assist you. You can say:

> *"I call on my trusted allies in spirit to assist me in clearing this space. Help me remove what does not belong and restore balance here."*

Always thank them when the work is done. Relationships are everything in spirit work.

EXERCISE: The Lesser Banishing Ritual of the Pentagram

The Lesser Banishing Ritual of the Pentagram (LBRP) is a foundational rite in ceremonial magic. Rooted in Hermetic and Kabbalistic traditions, this ritual is structured, layered, and deeply symbolic. While it wasn't part of my earliest intuitive practice, when I eventually explored ceremonial systems, I came to understand its power.

The LBRP is not just a tool for "banishing" unwanted energy from a space, it's a practice that clears and aligns the *practitioner*. It strengthens your energetic field, reinforces your spiritual sovereignty, and prepares you to act as a balanced vessel for any magical or spiritual work that follows. Through sacred names, visualization, and directional gestures, you invoke elemental and divine energies to center yourself in the ritual landscape.

If you're drawn to structure and symbolic precision, this ritual can become a powerful part of your daily practice. It's not required for spirit work, nor is it the only way to cleanse or protect yourself. But if you feel called to ceremonial frameworks, it can be incredibly transformative.

It's important to be discerning. While the LBRP can be a strong and effective banishing ritual, it's ceremonial at its core. Spirit work – at least as this book presents it – is accessible, intuitive, and rooted in lived experience. That doesn't mean it avoids complexity, but it does mean that not all systems translate fluidly across styles.

Including a full instructional breakdown of the LBRP would require accuracy, lineage understanding, and space. And while I honor this ritual and its practitioners, it's better placed in a book devoted to ceremonial magic, Western occult traditions, or as part of a dedicated magical training system.

That said, if you're curious, here's when you might explore the LBRP:

- When you need to do a thorough spiritual clearing of yourself or your space and lighter methods aren't effective.
- When you're working regularly with spirits and want a formalized method of establishing boundaries.
- If you're engaging in ritual magic that involves invoking or evoking spirits.

- When you're working within Western ceremonial systems, like Hermetic Qabalah or Thelema.

You'll find reputable instructions in traditional Golden Dawn texts, or from contemporary ceremonial magicians who honor its origins. If you do decide to learn the LBRP, treat it as a ritual discipline. Don't rush into it. Learn the meaning behind each word and gesture.

If the LBRP doesn't feel aligned with your path, however, that's okay. You don't need ceremonial banishings to have strong, effective boundaries. What matters is clear intention, consistency, and your relationship to the spirit world. Banishing can be deeply personal, rooted in your ancestry, your land, your guides. Use the tools that feel right. Create rituals that are living, breathing practices, which reflect your values and voice.

YOUR PROTECTIVE TOOLKIT

It's good to know when to apply protection in advance. For example, before a divination session, I might place a bowl of water by my workspace to absorb stray energies. If I'm visiting a place known for heavy history, I'll anoint myself with oil or carry protective herbs. If I feel I've already picked up something unpleasant, I'll do a cleansing bath or shower visualization to reset. Think of protection not as a single act but as a toolkit: preventive, active, and restorative. The more you practice, the more you'll know which layer of the toolkit to reach for.

PRACTICE SUMMARY

» Protection is less about fear and more about honoring your energy; reflect on how you create balance and safety in your life.

» Protective practices include rituals, talismans, offerings, and invocations; experiment to see which method resonates with you.

» Practice banishing energy with a firm voice and gesture: clap, stomp, or command "Leave now."

» Record your protective recipes or methods in a dedicated section of your journal for easy reference.

CHAPTER 9

Accessing the spirit realms

The spirit realms aren't "out there" in the way we often imagine them. They are layered with us, interwoven, parallel, and vibrating at different frequencies. Accessing these realms does not involve leaving your body or flying off into some distant astral place. You're shifting your perception, expanding your consciousness, and tuning your awareness to what already exists around you. We enter the spirit realms with intention, focus, and a grounded presence. Not with force or escapism, but attunement. This chapter explains how to access the spirit realms safely, consistently, and with reverence.

EXERCISE: Preparing the body and mind

Before entering your spirit space, your physical and energetic body must be calm, rooted, and present. While you don't need to be in a state of bliss, you should be anchored.

1. **Clear the space.** Light a candle. Burn cleansing herbs. Spray rose water. Let the area feel tended to.
2. **Unplug distractions.** Put your phone away. Let others in your home know you're not to be disturbed.
3. **Ground yourself.** Stand or sit with your feet on the floor. Take a few breaths. Let your awareness drop into your body. Wiggle your fingers. Settle.

4. **Set your intention.** Be specific. Are you journeying to meet a guide? Seeking insight? Simply opening and listening? Name your purpose.
5. **Call in support.** If you work with specific spirits or allies, this is the time to call them in. If not, ask simply for a benevolent presence to surround you.

You don't need elaborate rituals for this. But you do need consistency. The spirits you meet will take you more seriously when you show up with clarity and respect.

EXERCISE: Building and moving into the power

This is a foundational practice for stepping into spirit communication. You're not just waiting passively for something to happen, you're actively raising your energy, focusing your awareness, and inviting connection.

1. **Breathe and center.** Sit comfortably. Close your eyes. Begin to breathe deeply, in through the nose, out through the mouth. With each exhale, release tension. With each inhale, draw in presence.
2. **Build the power.** Now, begin to shift your awareness inward. Visualize a light within you, at your solar plexus, heart, or center. With every breath, allow it to grow. See it pulsing, expanding. This is your energy building.

3. **Feel the shift.** Your field becomes brighter. Your awareness sharpens. You are still grounded but now you're also elevated, your frequency rising. Let the energy move outward around your body, forming a gentle glow or aura. Sit with this.

4. **Invite spirit presence.** When you feel the energy strong and stable, say silently or aloud:

   "I am open to communication from loving, wise spirits aligned with my highest good. I am listening."

Use whatever language feels natural to you. Pause. Listen. Feel. You may sense temperature changes, a pressure shift, tingling, a sudden image, or a phrase that floats in. Stay present. Don't chase or force anything. This is a conversation, not a performance.

Shifting states of consciousness

To access the spirit realms, you must step outside of ordinary awareness to expand your perception of reality. This is not about entering a trance for spectacle's sake. It's about gently shifting into a receptive state where subtle impressions become clearer. You don't need to be a deep meditator or altered state expert. You just need openness and a willingness to soften your focus.

Once you've built power and set your intention, imagine yourself stepping through a doorway. It can be literal, like a gate in a garden, or abstract, like a veil or curtain. This image becomes your threshold between the physical and spirit space. Step through it slowly. Let your senses adjust. Spirit realms respond to presence, not urgency. You might feel a drop in temperature, a wave of emotion, or a subtle hum. These are cues that you're tuned in. Don't rush to label or decode everything. Let the experience unfold.

This practice may take five minutes or an hour. Some days will feel quiet. Others will feel vivid and full. All of it counts. Keep a journal nearby and write down what you see, feel, or sense – no matter how small.

Creating a safe energetic container

Working in the spirit realms without preparation is like opening your front door then walking away. You want to create boundaries that honor both you and the spirits you may encounter. Visualize a container around your space: a dome of light, ring of salt, or net of stars. Whatever resonates with you. This container is not meant to block or control; it simply holds the space with clarity. You might speak aloud:

> *"This space is sealed in light and intention. Only beings of love, wisdom, and truth may enter."*

Or you can whisper:

> *"Only what's aligned may cross this threshold."*

Let the container take shape around you. You may reinforce it with physical elements like stones, candles, or symbolic objects. What matters is your trust in its power.

It's important to normalize this process. Sometimes when reaching into the unseen, things feel murky, odd, or unsettling. This doesn't always mean danger; it might mean your own energy is off or that the timing isn't right. Pause. Ground again. Ask internally: *Is this aligned for me right now?* If the answer feels like a "no," thank the space and close it. Never push through resistance out of curiosity. There will be other opportunities. Spirit communication is a relationship, not a thrill ride.

We don't access the spirit realms to escape this one, but to deepen our relationship with reality by learning how to perceive more of it. These realms are not somewhere "out there" reserved for the gifted or initiated. They are layered into the world around us. And with practice, we learn to sense their presence, move toward them with respect, and return with clarity.

After building your energy and softening your awareness, the transition into spirit space may be subtle. It might feel like stepping into a dream, or standing in a quieter, more electric version of the room you're already in. You may notice colors appear brighter or sounds shift slightly. Time may stretch. You're not disconnected; you're attuned.

SLOW DOWN

One of the most effective ways to stabilize your connection with the spirit world is to slow down your internal pace. Let your breath guide you. Let yourself observe without needing to name or explain what you're experiencing. The more curious and open you remain, the more spirit realms can reveal themselves to you. It's okay if nothing happens at first. This work rewards presence, not performance. The more time you spend practicing, the easier it becomes to know when you're truly in the spirit realms or when your mind is simply trying to create something. Real contact often feels quieter, but more charged. It's like the air has shifted, or your chest tingles, or you suddenly feel deeply seen.

Always remember to close the space when you're done. Thank any spirits who showed up, either aloud or silently. You might feel drawn to blow out a candle, wash your hands, or physically step back from where you were sitting. These gestures help your body return fully to ordinary awareness. You may feel a bit fuzzy or tired after deeper work, and that's normal. Drink water, rest if you need, and write down your impressions. Over time, your spirit journal will become one of your greatest teachers.

Working in the spirit realms is not about perfection or control. You are building relationships, first with yourself then with the unseen. Each experience adds to your understanding, not just of spirit, but of your own intuitive capacity. You are not separate from these realms. You're already part of them. This practice is simply the remembering.

PRACTICE SUMMARY

- Begin with guided meditations or visualizations that carry you into an inner landscape.
- Identify a consistent "gateway" in your mind's eye (such as a door, staircase, or tree). Use it each time to enter.
- Practice short journeys first, returning after a few minutes.
- Journal your impressions and compare them across sessions; consistency strengthens access.

CHAPTER 10

Opening to channeling

Channeling is one of the most direct ways to connect with the spirit world. It is the process of allowing energy, impressions, or messages to flow through you, rather than trying to figure them out with your mind alone. Rather than performance or theatrics, it is about creating space for truth to move through you in a way that feels clear and safe. For many, the first signs of channeling are subtle: a sudden phrase that repeats itself in your mind, a shift in tone when you write in your journal, or a sense that words are being "handed" to you. With practice, these impressions become easier to recognize and trust.

To step into this work with clarity, you should understand the difference between psychic perception and mediumship. Psychics tune into energy, patterns, or impressions. Mediums connect directly with spirits who choose to communicate. Both abilities can overlap, but when you are channeling, knowing the source of the message helps you discern whether it is a symbolic impression, an energetic echo, or a direct communication. I touched briefly on this distinction in *Spirit World*, but in this book the goal is to move beyond explanation and into practice.

Channeling is about strengthening your relationship with spirit and learning how to trust the flow of information. You're not trying to prove anything to others. The following practices will help you begin opening the channel while also grounding your experiences so they remain balanced, safe, and useful in your daily life.

Channeling is one of those words that can mean different things depending on who you ask. Some people think of it as speaking in trance. Others think of it as automatic writing or downloading divine insight. And the truth is, it can be all of that.

In my own practice, I've come to understand channeling as a form of communication that often blurs the line between psychic perception and mediumship. It involves entering a receptive state, tuning your awareness like a radio dial, and allowing insight to come through from your higher self, guides, or a spirit energy outside of yourself.

If the energy you are channeling comes from a spirit who has passed on – a loved one, ancestor, or spirit ally – it falls under the umbrella of mediumship. If the energy comes from a guide, your intuition, or the broader collective consciousness, then it might be more psychic or intuitive in nature. It's less about hard definitions and more about noticing where the information is coming from and how it feels in your body and mind.

Channeling requires surrender without losing discernment. That means opening your awareness;

allowing words, images, or impressions to flow through but always remaining grounded enough to stay present. You don't need to "black out" or go into a trance to channel (though some do). You can be awake, aware, and still act as a conduit.

A simple way to begin practicing channeling is through writing. Sit quietly, ask a clear question or focus on a spirit you trust, and begin writing whatever flows without judgment. Don't overthink. Let the words come, and review them afterward. With time, you'll begin to sense when you're tapped into something beyond your own inner voice, and when you're just working something out on paper. Channeling is a practice of trust. And like all spirit work, it deepens with consistency, humility, and heart.

Channeling is a practice of presence, trust, and surrender. It doesn't require dramatic trance states or theatrical gestures. Often it's quiet. Subtle. A soft stream of insight flowing just beneath the surface of your thinking mind. And yet it can offer some of the most profound spiritual experiences you'll ever have.

MY OWN CHANNELING PROCESS

When I began channeling consciously, I realized it wasn't something entirely new. I'd already been doing it for years in softer ways. The times I spoke words I hadn't planned, that struck truth deep in someone's chest. The times I wrote pages of material that felt like they came through me, not from me. Or the many nights I dreamed of symbols and archetypes that later shaped the heart of my oracle decks. All of that was channeling.

One of the clearest examples came when I was creating my first oracle deck. I wasn't just designing artwork or writing messages, I was in conversation. The images, words, and structures didn't come from a business plan or content calendar. They came through dreams, intuitive nudges, or moments where I'd sit down to write and something else would take over. I could feel the presence of something ancient, supportive, and creative moving through me. I wasn't possessed. I wasn't out of control. I was attuned. I was listening. And I trusted what I heard.

If you're just starting with channeling, begin simply. Choose a method that grounds you, like journaling or voice recording, and give yourself a clear prompt. Ask something like: *What message is most needed right now?* Or: *Spirit, what do you want me to know today?* Sit quietly for a few moments, soften your breath, then begin writing or speaking without filtering. Let the words come even if they seem odd or out of place. Don't try to make it perfect. Don't worry if it sounds like you at first; most true channeled work carries your voice, but with an energy just beyond your usual mind. It helps to set a container. Light a candle. Call in your guides or protective spirits. You can say something like:

> *"I open with clarity and consent. I call in only energies and spirits aligned with truth, compassion, and my highest good. I am willing to receive what serves, and I release what does not."*

After your channeling session, ground yourself. Drink water. Journal anything you felt physically or emotionally. Review what came through and notice how it lands. Did something shift in your body? Did the message surprise you? Did it offer peace, clarity, or even challenge in a meaningful way? These are signs that you're not just thinking, you're receiving.

Over time, you may find that channeling becomes part of other areas of your work. Maybe it guides your art, spellwork, or healing practice. Maybe it's how you begin readings for others, or how you connect with your own guides. The key is to remain discerning and anchored. Not every impression is truth, and not every message needs to be shared. You'll know when something moves through you that feels alive, clear, and compassionate. Channeling is less about being chosen and more about choosing to listen.

Ways to communicate with spirits

Understanding whether an impression comes through psychic sensitivity or mediumship helps lay the groundwork for channeling. It clarifies how you receive information and what you can trust as you begin the practice. Psychics tune into subtle energies. Mediums act as a bridge for direct communication with spirits. While the roles can overlap, the distinction matters because channeling often draws on elements of both. Sometimes you may be receiving impressions or symbolic information (a psychic process). At other times, you may feel you are speaking or writing words on behalf of a spirit presence (a mediumistic process).

By noticing whether you are engaging psychically, mediumistically, or somewhere in between, you strengthen your discernment and develop trust in your own process.

Experiences may arrive quietly. Subtly. You might simply know something you haven't been told. You might feel a presence enter a room when no one else does. You might suddenly be flooded with emotion that doesn't belong to you. That's not imagination. That's awareness.

Psychic information tends to arise from within, from your own body or energetic field. Mediumship often feels like something external entering your awareness. Some mediums describe a shift in temperature, a pressure around the crown or third eye, or the sense of being "joined" by another presence.

If you're not sure where your strengths lie, begin by noticing. When you feel "tuned in," what's happening? Are you getting clear mental pictures? Emotional downloads? A whisper that isn't quite yours? The more you track these experiences, the more you'll understand how your system naturally receives and processes spiritual input.

PERSONAL REFLECTION: LEARNING TO TRUST MY IMPRESSIONS

One of the most pivotal points in my development came through my time studying with the Arthur Findlay College. I enrolled in several of their online courses. These virtual classrooms became sacred spaces where my intuitive muscles were tested, stretched, and strengthened. Sitting in circle with students from around the world, many of whom were complete strangers, taught me more about trust than any book could.

During one session, I was paired with someone I'd never met. We had just minutes to "tune in" and deliver any impressions that came. I was nervous but I focused, opened, and spoke honestly. The impressions that came were the image of a pocket watch, the scent of pipe tobacco, and a deep, unwavering sense of protection. Her eyes welled up. "That sounds like my grandfather," she said. "I have his pocket watch and his tobacco pipe."

Through moments like that, when my impressions were met with recognition and emotion, I began to trust the process. Not every reading landed perfectly, which was part of the learning too. But being able to replicate results and notice what felt energetically clear, versus what felt muddled or forced, was invaluable. Repetition, reflection, and feedback taught me how to discern between wishful thinking and true connection.

Equally important was the space to practice ethically, with permission and intention. The people I read for in the course knew they were part of a learning experience. Their consent created a container of safety, and their openness helped me see what was working. There's no substitute for that kind of practice, where you don't need to be "right" but are learning what alignment feels like, how connection unfolds, and how to listen with your whole being.

EXERCISE: Daily practice

To strengthen your psychic senses, start with a daily practice of stillness.

1. **Close your eyes, breathe slowly, and scan your body.** Notice any subtle shifts in temperature, pressure, or emotion. Begin asking yourself simple questions: *What do I feel right now? What energy is present in this room?* The goal is to tune into the subtle signals you're often too busy to notice.
2. **Keep a notebook nearby.** Record any impressions that arise: colors, images, sensations, or thoughts that feel out of place. Over time, patterns will emerge. You'll recognize when an insight comes from your intuitive self, and when it's your thinking mind.
3. **If you're leaning into mediumship,** try creating a sacred space before attempting contact. Dim the lights, light a candle, and spend a few minutes grounding your energy. Invite a benevolent spirit ally to draw near, not one you name, but one who has your highest good in mind. Speak aloud or in silence:

   > *"I open this space with respect. If there is a spirit who wishes to connect with clarity and integrity, I am ready to listen."*

4. **Then listen. Don't push.** Let your breath stay steady and your awareness open. If anything arises – a sudden memory, a wave of emotion, a particular scent or image – note it. Don't analyze it yet. Stay receptive.

5. **Afterward, journal what you experienced.** With practice, you'll learn to discern which impressions belong to spirit and which arise from your own internal world.

You can also practice blending both skills by sitting quietly with a friend. Ask them to think of a loved one in spirit or a situation they're dealing with. Then gently attune your awareness to what you feel. Speak your impressions without judgment. This is practice, not performance. The more you trust the process, the stronger the connection becomes. Whether psychic or mediumistic, the key is repetition. Respect. And rest. These abilities are natural but grow stronger with devotion. Let your daily practice be a ritual of attention. Your spiritual senses, like any others, come alive when given space to stretch and move.

PRACTICE SUMMARY

- Begin each session by grounding and centering, then invite clarity and truth before opening the channel.
- Keep a journal nearby and write freely without censoring; let impressions, words, or images flow even if they seem fragmented.
- Practice short sessions of automatic writing or speaking aloud to become familiar with the sensation of energy moving through you.
- Pause often to check in: ask yourself whether what you receive feels symbolic, intuitive, or like a direct spirit communication.
- Close each session intentionally with thanks then record any insights or patterns for reflection later.

CHAPTER 11

Building spiritual relationships

Like all relationships, spiritual relationships are built on trust, mutual respect, and time. Just as we wouldn't walk up to a stranger and expect them to bare their soul, we shouldn't expect instant connection or profound insight from a spirit we've never worked with before. The bonds develop slowly, shaped by consistency, communication, and reciprocity.

I remember when I began building a relationship with one of my ancestral guides. I didn't know who they were, only that their presence kept showing up during meditation. It was subtle: a scent, a sense of being watched, a particular phrase that wouldn't leave my mind. It took months of acknowledgment, offerings, and showing up at my altar before their energy became clear enough to name. That relationship didn't come with booming messages. It was like a whisper I kept listening to.

TRUST THE PROCESS

Whether you're connecting with an ancestor, deity, land spirit, or protective ally, the relationship is a process. Sometimes it begins with you reaching out; other times, the spirit reaches toward you. Both cases are an invitation.

> You are choosing to walk into something relational, not transactional. This means listening as much as asking. Offering as much as receiving. Checking in even when you don't want anything. These relationships become the framework for your spiritual practice, not because they grant you power, but because they teach you humility. They show you how to listen better. How to attune more clearly. How to honor the unseen with the same devotion you would show a trusted friend or teacher.

Part of balancing these spiritual relationships is acknowledging your own biases and projections. It's tempting to project what we want to see in a spirit, rather than how they actually present themselves. It's also easy to fall into old belief systems that categorize spirits as "good" or "bad" based on fear or cultural conditioning. But relationships ask more of us; they ask us to stay curious, question where our beliefs come from, and lean into nuance. True connection with spirits is mutual. It respects autonomy, both yours and theirs. It's about recognition, not control or manipulation. It's about aligning your energy with theirs in a way that fosters growth on both sides.

As your relationships with spirits deepen, so too will the complexity of your experiences. What begins as a quiet presence may evolve into dreams, omens, or clear messages during ritual. But just like with human connections, not every relationship will be lifelong. Some spirits walk with you for a season, specific purpose, or single teaching. When their role has been fulfilled, they may step back or disappear entirely.

This is not abandonment but alignment. Spirits often come into our lives to support a particular chapter of growth, healing, or transformation. When that chapter ends, the nature of the relationship may shift. It's important to honor that. Thank them. Acknowledge the gift of their presence, even if it felt fleeting.

Sometimes you may feel distance from a spirit you've known for years. Don't panic. Like any relationship, spiritual bonds ebb and flow. Instead of forcing connection, ask yourself: *What needs to change in me? Am I still approaching this with reverence? Am I listening as much as I'm speaking?* These moments of silence can be initiatory in themselves: an invitation to go inward, refine your intention, or deepen your practice. Also remember that not all spirits will feel warm or loving. Some come through with bluntness or challenge. Others feel stern. Some may seem indifferent. Just like a trusted mentor doesn't always sugarcoat their feedback, some spirits push you because they know what you're capable of.

Not every spirit interaction will feel comfortable. Your task is to discern: *Is this spirit aligned with my values? Is our exchange mutual, ethical, and rooted in respect?* If the answer is "yes," lean in even when it's not easy. If the answer is "no," or if the relationship feels extractive, draining, or violating, step back. You're allowed to say "no." You can end spiritual relationships, just as you would any that become harmful or misaligned. Spiritual boundaries are vital. They protect the integrity of your relationships and energetic well-being. They make space for discernment. Even in the unseen world, you have agency.

Just like in our physical lives, spiritual relationships thrive on reciprocity. It's easy to fall into the habit of asking spirits for guidance, protection, clarity, or help without offering anything in return. But true connection is built on mutual exchange. Ask yourself: *What am I giving back?* Offerings are one way to honor that exchange: gifts like water, flowers, incense, song, or even acts of service can speak volumes in spirit work. Offerings can also include time, devotion, presence, and consistency. Spirits recognize sincerity. They know when you show up with reverence, and when you're just checking boxes. Authenticity matters more than perfection. You don't need elaborate rituals to build strong relationships; you need intention, humility, and a willingness to grow.

Sometimes spirits will ask for something specific. You might feel a pull to visit a particular place, light a certain candle, speak a name, or sing a song. These requests often come through subtle intuition or repetitive signs. But this is where discernment is vital. Spirit does not demand harm to yourself or others. If a request feels unsafe, pause and reassess. Connection should never come at the cost of your well-being.

Certain spirits may feel more present at particular times of the year or in specific locations. For example, an ancestor may draw near during seasonal celebrations or personal milestones. A land spirit might become more responsive as you spend consistent time outdoors. Honor their timing. Relationships deepen over time and through rhythm. But you're not obliged to maintain relationships that feel out of alignment. Ending a connection can be just as sacred as beginning one. You can speak it aloud:

> *"I thank you for the time we've shared.*
> *Our paths are now parting. I release*
> *you with gratitude and respect."*

Burn an offering, close the space, and return to yourself.

Courting spirits

Some practitioners refer to the process of building a relationship with a spirit as *courting a spirit.* I love that phrasing. It invites us to move slowly, with reverence and warmth. Courting is about creating the conditions for connection to bloom. When you court a spirit, you open the door and invite them in, not as a servant or tool, but as an ally with agency, wisdom, and spirit of their own. The way you approach this will differ depending on the type of spirit you're connecting with.

Deities

When courting a deity, you might begin with research, myth, or a shared symbol. Create an altar or leave offerings known to resonate with that deity: wine, honey, incense, poetry. Speak their name with respect. Let them know you're open. Then wait. Watch your dreams. Listen for patterns. The response may be subtle or come with force. Either way, you'll know.

Land spirits

When courting land spirits or nature allies, your offering is presence. Regularly spend time in the same place. Bring small gifts like water, tobacco, flowers, or song. Speak aloud or simply sit with reverence. Ask permission before you work with the land. Introduce yourself each time until the space begins to feel like it knows you. These spirits may not speak in words, but respond to attention and care.

Ancestral spirits

When working with underworld or ancestral spirits, ritual and boundaries are key. Make your space clear, protected, and intentional. Ancestors may respond to food, candlelight, names spoken aloud, or songs they once knew. Underworld spirits may require deeper energetic preparation or protective measures. Don't rush into working with these energies. Move slowly, and only with consent and clarity.

Angels

When courting angels or ascended masters, the energy often feels higher, lighter, and more expansive. You might work with prayer, meditation, or sacred geometry. These beings often respond to purity of intention, calls for healing, and service-centered work. Call them in through light, sound, or devotional language. Be clear about your intention.

Building trust

Across all forms, the underlying principle is this: you're building trust. You're showing up not just to ask, but connect. Not just to receive, but be in relationship. Courting a spirit means taking your time. It means learning their stories, feeling into their presence, offering without expectation, and listening when they choose to speak. Just like in human relationships, not every spirit will feel like a match. That's okay. Not all doors will open. That's okay too. But when one does – when a spirit meets you with warmth, recognition, and clarity – you'll know. And what unfolds from there will become one of the most meaningful parts of your practice.

PRACTICE SUMMARY

- » Choose one spirit you've connected with and spend time building rapport; greet them daily at your altar.
- » Practice reciprocity: give an offering in exchange for insight or guidance.
- » Keep a record of promises made and whether they were fulfilled on both sides.
- » Reflect on the difference between fleeting encounters and long-term allies.

CHAPTER 12

Ways to communicate with spirits

For millennia, people of different cultures and groups worldwide have been petitioning and communicating with spirits. Although details like the type of food or scent of incense offered might vary, the core methods and formats in which people connect with spirits have remained. The Fox sisters' celebrity status helped launch the Spiritualist movement in the late nineteenth century. These three women communicated with spirits by asking questions and listening to rapping on the wall for answers. Today, communication from spirits comes to us in many ways, including signs, symbols, and dreams. It often involves some sort of exchange as a token of gratitude and recognition. While the fundamentals of independent spirit work are universal, individual beliefs – including desires, fears, needs, or level of compulsion and emotions – will affect the transaction's result.

Before you start practicing the different methods of communicating, let's revisit some basics:

- **Cleanse and set your intention before you begin.** Set the intent of connecting with only the energies you want to. A sacred space should always be clean and tidy before inviting new energies in. This ensures you've cleared out any unwanted energy, so you don't unintentionally connect to something less desirable. Use smoke, a cleansing wash, or choose your own favorite cleansing method before attempting contact with spirits.

- **Take precautions against any negative energies and entities.** Safeguarding against picking up unwanted entities and energies helps limit the negative influences they can have on our lives. It's always better to be safe than sorry, but you don't need to overdo it. Using your preferred protective methods in the appropriate way and with proper intention will always do the trick.
- **Be conscious of who you're connecting with.** Don't invite conversations with every spirit or entity. Although instances of contact with spirits who cause actual harm are rare, there are some who don't always consider your best interests. The best way to protect yourself from vulnerability is to state clearly who you are welcoming to connect with. If you feel uncomfortable or sense negative energy, tell them to leave firmly and politely. Setting boundaries will help provide you with self-preservation and keep any unwanted energies away. The longer you spend building your relationships,

the easier it is to recognize which spirits are loving and altruistic.

- **Use your common sense.** Don't purposefully put yourself in harm's way. Just like humans, spirits who care about us may not always tell us the truth. Sometimes spirits will keep things hidden for our own benefit or share incorrect information out of sincerity or concern. Keep using your discernment, critical thinking, and cross-checking skills. Whatever the case is, remember you are an intelligent person capable of recognizing misinformation and red flags. Continue to question things and be diligent about double-checking when you feel it's necessary.

Altars

Communication with spirits is unlimited. While some people inherit certain strengths with psychic abilities, others find meditating at a location of centralized energy conducive to their communicative efforts. Altars serve many purposes in various practices and traditions. In terms of communicating with spirits, creating an altar establishes a protective space to connect and exchange energy with spirits, which aids in building a strong, long-lasting relationship.

Altars can be elaborate or simple. Their purposes may vary; they could be a dedicated space to work with a spirit or for setting specific intentions and performing rituals. An altar's setup and appearance can vary as much as the practitioners who work with them. A successful altar contains items you connect with to represent or dedicate to certain energies, intentions, and spirits. The space in which you build an altar should feel comfortable and removed from distraction.

TENDING YOUR PORTAL

Altars serve as a portal for spirits and are a powerful way to build a clear channel of energy. Focusing intensely on the energy you wish to connect with at an altar can have positive results in manifesting outcomes. Consciously tending to your altar through petitioning spirits in exchange for your devotion encourages success. Furthermore, it can have tremendous benefits, as long as you remember to listen to your instincts and intuition.

Symbols and synchronicities

Signs are just one of the many forms through which spirits try to contact us and send us messages. Signs from spirits can include physical signs, symbols, or synchronicities. They can hold a vast potential of meanings, but they especially hold a significance to the person they're intended for.

You'll recognize signs because of your connection to them. Spirits often use items that resonate with you either consciously or subconsciously. Synchronicities are similar in the sense that you'll feel like something is familiar or a déjà vu kind of moment. A synchronicity is an occurrence of random events that appear to have relevant or significant meaning.

To receive signs from spirits that you have a connection with, be clear about your request and to whom, as well as what you will recognize as a sign. You can also tell spirits which items are important to you and ask them to provide a sign for guidance or clarity.

When something resembling a message comes your way, focus on your thoughts and what was happening at the time. The meaning might come to you later, or it might already be embedded into your subconscious to access later. Trust the messages that come through naturally, without trying to force meaning or shape them into something you want.

HELP WITH READING SIGNS

If you think you haven't received a sign, it may indicate that the meaning may not come to you instantly but later at a time when you need to access its meaning. Be patient – the meaning can come at any time, including minutes or weeks later. Spirits and the universe are constantly sending us signs. If you feel like you received a spiritual sign, but you're not entirely sure what it means, try this affirmation:

"I send my gratitude to spirit and the universe for this, and I release needing to know what it means at this time because its meaning will become clear to me when I need it."

With time and spiritual practice, certain symbols may start showing up in your dreams, meditations, or day-to-day life. Some of them may carry deeply personal meanings, while others seem to tap into a shared spiritual language that crosses cultures and beliefs. Here are some symbolic impressions I've encountered in my own practice and in experiences shared by others. Keep in mind that symbols are fluid; they speak in feeling, timing, and intuition more than fixed definitions. What matters most is what they mean to you at the moment you receive them.

- **Roses** may point to themes of unconditional love, reconciliation, or a spirit presence offering peace.
- **Rainbows** often arrive as spiritual affirmations, signs of alignment, emotional healing, or renewal after a difficult period.
- **Birds in flight** can symbolize soul communication, freedom, or messages from beyond.
- **Keys** may suggest an opportunity becoming available, or a breakthrough in clarity or direction.
- **Candlelight** tends to symbolize spiritual presence or an invitation to slow down and connect more intentionally.
- **Stars** are sometimes seen as ancestral signs or divine timing, especially when they show up in dreams or visions.

- **Coins or feathers** found unexpectedly may point to ancestral support or small signs that you are not alone.
- **Mirrors** can represent self-reflection, hidden truths, or the presence of a spirit encouraging clarity.
- **Rain or storms** might symbolize emotional processing or a buildup of unresolved energy.
- **Butterflies or moths** are commonly linked to transformation, the spirit world, or messages from departed loved ones.
- **Animals**, especially those seen repeatedly, can carry messages unique to their nature: an owl for wisdom, a fox for discernment, or a deer for gentleness and grace.
- **Books** or handwritten letters might represent untold stories, insight arriving, or a message seeking to be understood.
- **White or golden light** often accompanies high-vibration spirits or healing energy.
- **Dark clouds or thick fog** can indicate confusion, grief, or a moment of spiritual recalibration.

- **Fire or flames** may symbolize purification, passion, or spirit energy that brings change or release.

Trust the feeling that arrives with a symbol more than logic. Sometimes the meaning is instant; other times it unfolds gradually. The more you welcome these moments without overthinking them, the clearer their messages become. Keep a running list in your journal of recurring signs and what they've meant for you. Over time, you'll build a symbolic language that is deeply personal and surprisingly accurate.

Meditation

Meditation is vital and necessary to access the door to the other side. The first rule of thumb is this: there is no single or correct way to meditate. The most beneficial environment to establish accurate and strong connections with spirits is a state of relaxation. Relaxation establishes the necessary receptivity to connect clearly with spirits and energies. Meditation methods vary from using dance, movement, and drum beats to practicing stillness and breathwork. Try as many as possible to see which format suits you best for getting into a meditative state. The goal of meditation is to create a space in the mind for clarity. Meditation can be the means to bring you answers as well as provide the foundation to meet spirits.

Prior to commencing your meditation, state your desired outcome. You can do this as a prayer, or simply by stating, "With this meditation, I seek to … [state your intention]." Then begin your meditation by your preferred method. A plethora of guided meditations are available online that are great for beginners.

When my overactive mind won't allow me to get into a meditative state, grounding or performing some sort of active movement and exercise helps to expel excess energy before I begin. I've also enjoyed entering meditative states while walking or dancing. You'll want to choose somewhere that is comfortable and free from any distractions. To support this, try things like diffusing lavender essential oil, using calming crystals like lepidolite, lighting candles, or wearing comfortable clothing. These help quiet the conscious mind of impeding thoughts so you allow for your answers to come through clearly. Work on achieving a state of relaxation – the state right before you enter sleep – by any methods that work for you. This state cannot be achieved through force. Although it's nearly impossible to relinquish and subdue all impeding thoughts, just allow for them to come then pass.

TROUBLE-SHOOTING YOUR PRACTICE

If you're having trouble meditating, ask yourself: *What helps me to get into a state of relaxation? Is it listening to calming sounds and music? Is it counting down from 1,000?* Do what works for you. Regular practice will help strengthen your skill and better understand the place you are trying to get to in your mind. Don't chase thoughts. When you are completely relaxed, witness them entering your mind and allow them to pass. What images do you see? What do you hear? The messages and answers you seek can enter your mind in various different ways. Simply accept that the answer you are looking for is here, without wishing but knowing it to be.

Automatic writing

This is used to produce words without using the conscious mind. Automatic writing uses the unconscious energies through a practitioner's or medium's hand and arm to communicate. As you hold the pen or pencil over the paper, your hand will make small movements. These will cause marks on the paper. At first, these marks are just swirls and lines. Over time, they become more and more consecutive, forming letters and words.

Automatic writing can be done virtually anywhere. For example, just sit down with a sheet of paper while you read a book or watch television.

You can use this form of spiritual contact to connect directly with the spirits and write down messages from them. The writing will often appear in the spirit's handwriting style. You'll want to focus your mind on something else entirely while doing it. This will allow your hand to write a message without focusing on what is being written. Some people believe that using your nondominant hand is better for automatic writing.

To channel a message from a spirit, you need to enter a light trance state. Use trance triggers such as incense or shamanic drumming. Protect yourself by creating a space that only one spirit can enter at a time.

Pathworking

A type of meditation, pathworking allows you to experience the spirit world psychically while still tied to your physical body. Pathworking is a process where you follow a path that leads to the spirit world and back to where you came from. The key elements are a clear entrance and exit point, making it easier for your consciousness to return. It can be anywhere. You can use a door, tree, cave, or mountaintop. What's most important is that it's a recognizable and easy-to-find path back. Before you start a journey, make a rough road map. This will help you identify your goal, entry/exit point, and a general idea of where you're going. Pathworking is relatively beginner friendly and is often easier to perform than other meditations like astral travel. I recommend starting with it before trying astral travel.

How to journey with pathworking:

- **Establish a goal and a rough road map.** You can use a candle to purify the room or a ritual broom to sweep away old energy.
- **Sitting or lying down can help you start meditating.** You can also use music or breathing techniques to help you reach a state of deep relaxation. Once you've reached a meditative state, you'll see yourself standing at an entry point into the astral realm.

- **Return to the entry/exit point.** When you've completed your journey or your question is answered, return to where you arrived. This will help you return to your physical state. Once you are fully aware and back on the physical plane, remember to use a grounding method. If you choose, record your pathworking experience to reflect on later.

EXERCISE: Building your astral temple

For this exercise, we'll be working with benevolent spirits and asking your spirit guides to come close and meet you in your astral temple. This is a space that exists in a subtle, nonphysical realm where spiritual energies and entities reside. People use numerous terms to describe a sacred space or meeting place in the etheric realm meant for connecting with spirit guides. It's important not to get caught up on the specific terminology. What matters most is the intention and purpose behind creating such a space, a place where you can connect with spiritual guides and energies beyond the physical realm.

Once you are comfortable and confident with this exercise, feel free to customize it with guidance from your intuition. The options are endless, just make it personal. If you choose to provide a physical offering like food or water, place it in its offering dish or on the altar when you begin. If it's an energetic offering, state out loud what it is and who it's for.

1. **Begin the meditation either in a seated position or lying down.** Make sure you can move around freely later on. Close your eyes and take a few deep breaths, feeling the air enter and exit your lungs. As you breathe, feel the lower part of your body relaxing and releasing all tension, starting with your feet. Moving upward, feel your legs and hips relax. Breathe in and feel your calves release any tension. Relax your chest and back, focus on your breathing, and allow the neck to relax and the muscles in your face and head to release as well.
2. **Once your body is in complete relaxation, picture yourself outdoors in nature.** You may be surrounded by a field or in a forest. Appreciate all the beauty of the scenery around you. Relax into a sense of comfort, calmness, and safety in this place.
3. **Focus on your root energy center at your spine's base.** Visualize the energy spinning in a ball, emitting a deep red color. Take a few deep breaths. Place your focus on your sacral energy center, right in the center of your lower belly and back, just below the navel. Watch the orange ball of energy swirling in you. Breathe in and focus on your solar plexus energy center near your diaphragm. Feel the energy move and spin in a yellow array.
4. **Breathe into your heart center.** Allow your heart energy center to expand into the green circle of energy. See the green color of this energy vibrate faster and faster. Pay attention to your throat energy center. Watch the shades of blue spin as they appear.

5. **Focus on the energy from your third-eye energy center.** This is located between the eyebrows. Feel it grow and increase. Take a few moments to watch it, seeing its movement quicken. Visualize the crown energy center at the top of your head as the ball of white light glows, diffuses, and flows into your brain. Take a moment and enjoy the feeling of all these energy centers vibrating, churning, and pulsing energy.
6. **Guide your attention back to your location in nature.** You find a path to walk along and some steps to climb. Count them as you climb – one, two, three, four – continue counting until you arrive at a clearing. This is where you will construct your inner sacred space. Use your intuition as your guide. Visualize the materials appearing as you build.
7. **Get up from your position and find some space.** Go through the motions of building walls and windows. Your space may look however you like; it can be a cottage with a thatch roof, a midcentury modern house, a secret garden with ancient vines and ferns. This is your sacred space. You may also enter this space with the intention to find peace and clarity.
8. **Create a door that only you will be able to enter.** Imagine this as a strong door to enter and exit your space that only you have the key for. Next, create a door for others. This door is for all other entities and energies that you invite. It may be modern and made of glass, or old and ornately carved. Again, it is your preference.

9. **Install a light above your guest door.** This light will allow those who are aligned with your highest good to enter your space. The light shines brightly on all who stand at the guest door of your space and serves as the gatekeeper, defending your space from anyone with ill intent.

10. **Take a moment to sit in your sacred space.** Feel the positive energy that flows through with peace and clarity. Once you are ready and feel a state of calmness and clarity, state your intentions. Mentally or verbally call out to the archetype or your spirit guides, giving them permission to meet and state what it is you want:

    "I wish to connect with and communicate with my spirit guides.

    Only energies of the light and of the highest compassion may enter.

    Spirit guides, I ask for your guidance.

    You have my gratitude and appreciation for ... [name what it is you seek].

    In return, you have my respect, love, and devotion."

11. **Open the portal.** With your eyes closed, allow for visions of a being entering through the door, coming closer to you and manifesting. Your guides will enter into your sacred space, passing through the light above the door. Feel the immense love as they enter. As you witness these beings coming closer through the light of the door, recognize and notice thoughts but don't follow them. Focus on your breath.

12. **Pay attention.** Listen to any images, conversations, words, or sounds that occur. You may hear things in your own voice or from someone unrecognizable; listen to them and witness without force. Pay attention to your senses. What do you hear? What do you see? There may be messages provided to you.
13. **Enjoy your time with them and listen.** Give them time to provide you with what you've asked for. When you feel you are ready to say farewell, thank them with your love, appreciation, and gratitude. You may watch them leave through the guest door, or you may invite them to stay. Be absolutely sure you know who they are and what their intentions are if you ask them to stay.
14. **Exit your sacred place.** Go through your door and shut it behind you. Walk across the clearing and down the steps back to your original location surrounded by nature. Feel your consciousness returning to your physical body, and when you are ready to wake up, open your eyes.

Now that you have created your astral temple, you can use it whenever you wish. To come back to it, imagine sitting in a safe and comfortable place of nature. Meditate on your energy centers, then follow the path and step into your space. Use this space as somewhere you can connect with your intuition, meet loving spirits, aid in healing, and provide you with life's answers. When you feel ready, you'll exit through your special door. Over time, your space may change in appearance; however, it will always be available to you.

Once you have cultivated a space to meet your spirit guides and build a relationship, you can easily return to your space for their love and guidance. After you have worked to build and maintain a relationship with them, you can follow the path to your special sacred place in your mind. Later, ask your spirit guides to bring forth other spirits to communicate with you.

EXERCISE: Astral projecting

Once you are comfortable with pathworking, can reach deep meditative states, and have mastered things like lucid dreaming, you are ready to astral travel. Also known as spirit flight, astral travel is when you send your consciousness into the spirit world.

To begin, try to see your inner self (your etheric body) that travels during meditation; it's a more transparent version of you. Visualize it lifting up and out of the physical body. This step can be challenging, but it can help you feel more connected to your etheric body. After connecting with your etheric or astral body, set a goal or destination in mind for your astral journey. This could be anything from meeting a spirit guide to exploring a place. It can also include traveling to the past or future.

People sometimes use triggers to enter astral travel. A trigger is something to help release consciousness from the physical body. Triggers include things like music, chanting, or dancing. For instance, shamans frequently use drumming as their trigger to achieve spirit flight. It may take many attempts to find your appropriate trigger and learn how to have control over your astral body to follow your intention. Use energetic cleansing and grounding techniques after astral projecting to avoid picking up any unwanted entities. The more you practice, the easier it becomes.

EXERCISE: Astral projecting: the rope technique

An effective technique to aid in this process is the rope technique. Find a quiet and comfortable space where you can relax without interruptions. Create a soothing atmosphere with soft lighting and calming music if desired.

1. **Lie down or sit in a comfortable position.** Ensure your body is fully supported. Close your eyes and focus on deep, steady breaths to calm your mind. Release any physical tension by consciously relaxing each part of your body, starting from your toes and working your way up to your head. Visualize yourself floating or rising above your body, setting a clear intention to explore the astral realm or connect with spiritual guides.
2. **Visualize a strong, vibrant rope hanging above you.** See it extending upward into the cosmos. Feel its texture, notice its color, and mentally reach out to grasp it with your astral hands. As you hold onto the rope, feel its

solidity and allow yourself to slowly and steadily pull your astral body upward, away from your physical form. Imagine the sensation of your astral self ascending the rope, moving effortlessly through space.

3. **Feel your consciousness shift.** You may begin to feel subtle energies or vibrations throughout your body. This state often signifies a shift in consciousness to a vibrational state as you prepare to leave the physical body behind. Trust in the process and maintain focus on the sensation of climbing the rope, maintaining a calm and relaxed state of mind.

4. **Continue to ascend.** As you continue to ascend, you may notice sensations of weightlessness or movement. This indicates your astral body's separation from your physical form. Once fully detached, explore the astral realm with curiosity and openness. Observe landscapes, interact with entities, or seek guidance from spiritual guides.

5. **Return to your physical form.** When you're ready to return to your physical body, gently guide your awareness back. Visualize yourself descending along the rope. Feel the connection between your astral and physical bodies growing stronger as you approach your physical form. Gradually reintegrate by focusing on your breath and physical sensations, allowing yourself to fully reconnect with your body.

6. **Reflect on your experience.** Journal any insights gained during your journey. Each practice session with the rope technique enhances your ability to navigate the astral realm and deepen your spiritual connection. Remember, patience, practice, and a sense of exploration are essential as you embark on this transformative path of consciousness exploration.

Animal spirit guides

Many cultures have traditions that involve the protection and guidance of an animal spirit. If you want to meet your animal spirit before embarking, make sure you set an intention of working toward meeting your animal guide through pathworking. There are many factors to consider when choosing an animal guide. Know that you aren't choosing a guide that you already know or like. Your animal guide is an important part of your spiritual journey because they are capable of protecting and uplifting you. They may also help you in meeting other spirits or lead you to things you may need.

Offerings

There are thousands of spirits and deities, and who you choose to honor will often depend on what path you follow. Some deities are associated with specific aspects of the human experience such as love and marriage. Other spirits are associated with the phases and cycles of the planets and preside over seasons. Learning about the different gods and goddesses can help to identify which one would be the best fit for you to work with.

In actuality, offerings are not only for deity worship; you can give them to all kinds of spirits, including ancestors or land spirits. Not only can offerings be used for honoring them, showing appreciation and devotion, they can help pacify spirits or provide amends for accidental offense. Offerings can be provided physically or energetically and have a great power of influence or effect in gaining spiritual allies. You'll notice that physical offerings usually still remain after being given. It's rare that a spirit will have the power to consume them on the physical plane, but some spirits can feed off the smoke when we burn substances like plants or incense. If a physical offering is provided, such as food or drink, you can multiply its power through mental focus and create energetic variations.

You don't always need to leave out offerings in a ritualistic manner. They can be casually gifted and mentally provided for spirits in a plethora of settings. You may wish to recite a poem or passage that helps identify an offering as such. The important thing is that you make your intentions of your offering known. No matter how big or small the offering, attaching positive intent and providing them regularly will increase the chances of forming and building strong bonds with spirits.

In paganism and Wicca, practitioners may honor a god or goddess of one tradition or several. Sometimes they may ask for help with magical tasks or in solving problems. In many traditions, it's common for people to offer a sacrifice to the gods. One of the many issues that people tend to discuss when learning about worship is the topic of proper veneration. This concept states that we should treat deities with respect and honor them appropriately when taking the time for acts of worship, like making offerings. This is not a matter of requesting and having wishes fulfilled, but wanting to acknowledge their existence and show how much we appreciate their influence.

HOW DO YOU KNOW WHAT TO OFFER?

It can be difficult to find enough clear and explicit information on a spirit's favored offering or acts of devotion. In this case, how will you know what is an appropriate offering? Deities will respond differently depending on what offering you give. This is where research is essential. For example, Athena is a war goddess who was born in full battle armor. She is a powerful and primeval spirit. It is believed that war cries excite her. Some associate Athena with Neith, an Egyptian goddess who the ancient Greeks adopted and turned into Athena after traveling across the Mediterranean. She is petitioned for nearly anything. Appropriate offerings to consider would be something associated with her mythos. Because she is also a goddess of crafts, specifically weaving, offering her the fruits of your creative labor may be better received than something like flowers, which would be better suited to offer Aphrodite, the Greek goddess of love and beauty.

> Learning about a spirit or deity's myths and strengths can help you determine their preferences. It is important to consider what they represent. Aside from what the gods represent to you, you should also pay attention to what they have asked of others in the past. Taking the time to learn about a deity shows you how to worship them. If they represent love, for instance, what kinds of things could you offer? Examples might include roses, love letters, chocolates, candles, or incense – items that are often tributes of love. When in doubt, wine and bread are universally accepted, as well as clean water and milk. Ultimately, listen to your instincts and record what items provide you with the best response.

Rituals

A ritual is a ceremony that involves specific actions or words. Rituals can be performed in a specific manner or created to a specific cultural or religious origin. The rise of consciousness and spiritual embodiment has brought a resurgence in the explorations of conscious rituals. A ritual is a way to set the tone and vibration of energy through various actions. A ritual that includes intention-setting helps you acknowledge and elevate your manifestation. It also communicates to the universe that you are dedicated to being a deliberate creator. A ritual can be a space of renewal and retraining, carrying the energy of commitment, integrity, and trust.

Creating a ritual can be an important step in communicating with spirits. It allows us to consciously set intentions and receive them. An intention is a way of communicating with the universe. Think of it like a conscious and well-considered call to action. A clear and consistent intention is a reminder of what you are creating. It can also serve as a guide to your path. You can set intentions either silently or verbally. We often set intentions all day long. Even making a list of things to do can be viewed as a basic form of intention-setting. Creating a clear intention to receive certain emotions can help you experience these feelings throughout the process.

You can perform a ritual in many ways; it's up to you to decide how you want to create it. The most basic things needed are a quiet private space, a journal and pen, and being fully present. Creating a space that is designed to accommodate the ritual and its components is an important step when preparing for a powerful intention-setting. Be fully present in the moment, both physically and mentally. This is a time to be open to creativity and higher self-guidance. Accepting and working through difficult situations is the best way to move forward. Allow time and space to work through any spontaneous events that may arise when you are creating a ritual, rather than during the ritual itself.

It is important to decide what elements of your ritual you would like to include. You can also combine elements of different rituals and add extra details as you feel called to. For instance, if you feel compelled, you may include things like divination in your rituals, or artistic movement like dancing. The choices are endless and entirely yours – customize the ritual in alignment with your intuition. Each ritual is powerful because it is unique with its own characteristics.

EXERCISE: Creating your ritual for spirit connection

1. **Prepare your space.** Find a quiet and comfortable space where you feel safe and undisturbed. Clear the area of clutter and distractions. You may wish to cleanse the space with incense or a ritual bell to remove any lingering energies and create a sacred atmosphere.

2. **Set your intention.** Clarify why you wish to connect with spirits. It could be for guidance, healing, understanding,

or any other purpose. Your intention should be heartfelt, respectful, and aligned with your highest values and intentions.

3. **Gather your tools.** Select objects that hold personal meaning and resonate with you spiritually. This might include candles, crystals, herbs, photographs of loved ones who have passed, or any other items that evoke a sense of connection to the spirit realm.
4. **Create sacred symbols.** Arrange your chosen objects in a way that feels meaningful to you, whether on your altar or in any dedicated spiritual space. For example, place candles in a circle to represent the eternal cycle of life and death, or arrange crystals to amplify your intention and energy.
5. **Invoke spiritual presence.** Begin your ritual by calling upon specific spirits, spirit guides, ancestors, or deities whom you wish to connect with. You may do this through prayer, meditation, chanting their names, or simply speaking aloud your invitation with sincerity and respect.
6. **Open yourself to receive.** Close your eyes and focus on your breath to center yourself. Allow yourself to enter a receptive state of mind and heart. Become attuned to subtle energies and impressions. Be patient and open to whatever forms of communication may arise: feelings, thoughts, symbols, or intuitive insights.
7. **Communicate and listen.** Engage in conversation or silent communion with the spirits. Ask questions, seek guidance, or simply listen with an open heart. Trust your intuition and the messages that come through. Take note

of any thoughts, feelings, or images that resonate deeply with you.

8. **Express gratitude and release.** When you feel ready to conclude the ritual, thank the spirits for their presence and any messages received. Honor the connection you've established. Gently release the energy you've raised by thanking the spirits once more and visualizing any remaining energy returning to its source.
9. **Close the ritual.** Extinguish candles, tidy up your space, and ground yourself to close the ritual. Visualize roots extending from your feet into the earth, anchoring you firmly. Take a few deep breaths to integrate the experience and reflect on any insights gained.
10. **Reflect and journal.** After the ritual, take time to reflect on your experience. Write down any messages, feelings, or insights that arose during the ritual. Journaling can deepen your connection and understanding of the spiritual realm.

Remember, your personal ritual for connecting with spirits is unique to you and should reflect your spiritual beliefs and intentions. Trust your intuition, follow your heart, and let yourself explore and grow in your spiritual practice.

PETITIONING PRACTICE

One of the most effective ways to petition spirits is through writing. Take a blank piece of paper and write a simple, respectful request in the present tense. For example:

"I welcome clarity in my dreams tonight. Spirit allies, please bring insight that helps me move forward."

Fold the paper toward yourself to draw energy in, then place it under a candle, crystal, or symbol of your choice. Let it rest until you feel the petition is answered or complete, then thank the spirits and dispose of the paper respectfully, such as by burning or burying it. Small rituals like this turn your abstract intention into embodied action.

PRACTICE SUMMARY

- Practice three forms of communication: journaling impressions, asking yes/no questions with a pendulum, and observing omens in daily life.
- Write a short petition (clear, polite, and specific) and place it under a candle. Observe the results.
- Practice listening: spend five minutes in silence after a petition, noting your subtle impressions.
- Compare outcomes across different methods and decide which feels most reliable for you.

CHAPTER 13

Tools and techniques for divination

At its core, divination is about listening. Divination is the act of reaching toward mystery and allowing it to respond in symbols, sensations, and signs. In the context of spirit work, divination is not fortune-telling or prediction; it's relationship. It's the language we use to understand the presence and perspective of spirit. It's also how spirits may speak back.

While some forms of divination are passive – opening yourself to receive signs or symbols without asking a direct question – others are active, involving tools and direct inquiry. Both can be sacred. Both can be powerful. Neither should be rushed.

YOUR INTENTION MATTERS

What makes divination effective isn't just the tool, but the intention behind the question, the clarity of the seeker, and the openness to receive an answer that may challenge you.

When used regularly and with sincerity, divination becomes a kind of mirror. It reflects where your energy is, what spirit might be offering you, or what needs attention before you move forward.

Before practicing any form of divination, ground yourself. Set the space with a few deep breaths, a spoken or silent intention, and an openness to hear what needs to be heard. Ask clearly. Be specific. Be honest. Spirit responds best to sincerity.

Pendulum work

The pendulum is one of the first divination tools people turn to because of its simplicity. But don't underestimate it. In the right hands, the pendulum is a fine-tuned channel, responsive, nuanced, and deeply intuitive.

Start with a pendulum that feels right to you. It doesn't need to be made of crystal; it just needs to feel balanced in your hand and responsive when held still. Cleanse it when you first bring it home: smoke, salt, moonlight, or intention are all good options.

Hold it still between your thumb and forefinger. Ask aloud or silently, "Show me yes." Observe how it swings. Then ask, "Show me no." Make sure you can tell the difference. You might also ask it to show you "maybe" or "not now." Don't rush the process. Over time, your pendulum will speak in clearer ways. You can use the pendulum to:

- ask yes/no questions in spirit communication
- locate blocked or imbalanced energy
- determine whether it's the right time for a particular working
- confirm if an object, space, or spirit is aligned with your intention.

Some practitioners use pendulum boards with letters, numbers, or specific symbols. This is an advanced technique, what matters first is trust. Build your relationship with the pendulum the way you would with any spirit ally: slowly, respectfully, and with repetition.

Scrying

This is the art of gazing into a reflective surface to receive visions, impressions, or messages. Scrying requires patience. It asks you to sit with ambiguity. In those still, liminal moments, however, images and feelings often rise to the surface in surprising clarity. You can scry with:

- a black mirror
- a bowl of water
- candle flames
- smoke or incense trails
- crystals with a reflective sheen (like obsidian or clear quartz).

Here is a way to practice scrying. Dim the lights. Light a candle or place yourself in low light. Gaze softly at the surface, not focusing too hard or trying to force an image. Breathe deeply. Let your awareness drift. It may take several sessions before you receive anything distinct, but over time, impressions begin to form. You may see faces, symbols, colors, or shifting light. You may feel rather than see. Record what you receive in a journal, even if it seems random at first. Spirits may use this method to gently offer insight or nudge you in a new direction.

Casting tools: Bones, shells, stones, and charms

Casting is an ancient and intuitive form of divination that asks you to read the language of placement, pattern, and position. It requires no formal structure, but asks you to be deeply present – to trust what falls, where it falls, and how it feels. Traditionally, people used bones, shells, stones, seeds, or personal trinkets, whatever they had on hand that carried spiritual resonance. Each item had its own voice, its own story. Over time, people built and inherited sets.

If you're creating your own casting set, choose pieces that feel charged with meaning. A small animal bone, a coin, a river stone, a button, a charm shaped like a key or a heart. Keep the set small to start, between five and thirteen items is a manageable beginning. You can add or swap pieces later based on the messages you're receiving. To cast, center yourself. Ask your question clearly. Hold the pieces in your hands and let them drop onto a cloth or into a shallow bowl. Observe. Notice groupings, directions, spacing, and which items land face up or hidden beneath others.

There are no fixed rules for interpretation. Some people assign meanings to each item, while others read situationally. If a shell representing intuition lands far from the others, maybe there's emotional distance from your inner truth. If a coin lands close to a bone, maybe your energy is too tied to the physical or financial. With practice, casting becomes a dance between your subconscious and the spirit world, a way for unseen things to take shape.

Runes and symbols

More than just symbols etched into stone or wood, runes are echoes of an old language that still hums with power. Each rune carries layers of meaning: a sound, image, word, or spell. While runes are most often associated with Norse tradition, similar symbolic alphabets and sigil-like scripts have emerged across cultures. More than just tools of divination, they are keys that unlock something much older within us.

You don't need to be a scholar to use runes in spirit work. You just need to approach them with humility and care. Start with a small set if you feel called, perhaps focusing on a few that resonate with you. You can pull one rune at a time to gain insight or cast a handful and see how they fall. Runes can be burned into wood, painted on river stones, or drawn on paper. This can include making your own runes or working with ones you already have. When working with them, feel into the textures. Hold them. Breathe with them. Let them tell you their story. Spirit often uses symbols – they bypass logic and go straight to the gut, the soul.

Ask your question. Draw a rune. Close your eyes. Let the symbol echo in your mind. Is there a sensation, memory, or message rising? Write it down. Let it unfold slowly, like a dream you're just waking up from.

Cartomancy: Reading with tarot, oracle, or playing cards

Cards are structured, symbolic, and rich with archetype, which makes them one of the most accessible and layered forms of divination. Tarot especially offers a full narrative system: journey, challenge, transformation, and insight. While freer in format, oracle cards are often just as powerful. When working with cards for spirit communication or guidance, remember that it's not just about reading the cards. You need to listen to what's beneath them. How you feel when you see the imagery, what words echo in your mind, and how spirit might be nudging you to look closer.

Before drawing cards, ground yourself. Take a breath and center. Ask your question clearly, either aloud or in your heart. Shuffle with intention. Stop shuffling when it feels right. Draw your card or cards. You might use a single-card draw for daily insight or a more complex spread for spirit-led questions. The following is a simple but powerful spirit guidance spread, adaptable for tarot or oracle decks:

Card 1. What spirit or energy is present with me right now?

Card 2. What message or guidance is being offered?

Card 3. How can I best work with or honor this presence?

After pulling the cards, sit with them. Write down your impressions. Rather than rushing to interpret them based on the guidebook, feel into what each card says to you intuitively, then compare with the traditional meanings if needed. Often, spirit speaks in the space between what we expect and what we feel.

EXERCISE: A spirit work spread for oracle or tarot

When you want to consult your cards specifically about spirit work – seeking guidance from a guide, confirmation of presence, or clarity on the next step in your development – use this custom spread. You can use tarot or oracle cards for this spread. Light a candle, set a clear intention, and shuffle your deck slowly. Lay the cards as follows:

Card 1. Who is stepping forward in spirit right now?

Card 2. What is their message or guidance for me?

Card 3. What is the nature of our connection?

Card 4. What do I need to offer or acknowledge to deepen this work?

Card 5. What is the best next step on my path with spirit?

Let each card be a conversation. Speak aloud if it feels right. If something's unclear, pull a clarifying card or sit with it longer. You might feel warmth, pressure, emotion, or intuitive nudges as you read. That's your signal that something real is moving through.

Automatic writing and spirit dictation

Automatic writing is one of the simplest, most revealing ways to let spirit speak. It's also one of the most underestimated. There's a raw, unfiltered magic in putting pen to paper and letting the words flow. You don't need to wait for clarity or edit as you go. You don't even need to understand what's coming through in the moment.

- **Create a quiet space.** Light a candle or do a brief grounding ritual if it helps you drop in. Then pick up your pen and ask your question either aloud or silently. Try these general prompts: "Spirit, what would you like me to know right now?" or "What message is waiting to come through?"

- **Start writing.** Don't pause to think. Don't stop to correct spelling or grammar. Let the words move through you as if you're channeling a stream. Even if what comes out feels strange, incomplete, or messy, trust the process.
- **Later, read it back with gentle curiosity.** You may find guidance, phrases that feel wiser than your own voice, or even repetitions of symbols or themes that match other forrns of divination you've done.

Automatic writing is especially useful when you feel blocked, uncertain, or disconnected from your intuitive senses. It helps clear the channel and build trust between you and your spirit guides.

Dreamwork as divination

Your dream space is a spirit realm. Every night, you enter a landscape shaped by your subconscious, your soul, and sometimes the spirits who walk with you. Paying attention to your dreams is a sacred act of listening. Spirit often speaks loudest when your waking mind is quiet.

If you're not already tracking your dreams, start keeping a notebook beside your bed. The moment you wake – even if it's 3 a.m. – write down whatever fragments you remember. Don't worry if it's incomplete or strange. Write it anyway.

When spirit uses dreams to communicate, the messages can be symbolic, emotional, or direct. Repeating symbols (such as water, animals, doors) may be keys to specific energies. If you dream of someone you've lost or a being you don't recognize, note how you felt in their presence. Was it peaceful? Heavy? Empowering?

Before sleeping, you can also invite spirit guidance:

> *"Spirit, if there's something I need to know, I'm open to receiving it in my dreams tonight."*

It doesn't always work right away, but your dream body becomes more responsive over time. In the dream world, timelines dissolve. Spirit allies, ancestors, and archetypes often appear in ways we wouldn't expect. Honor what shows up. Ask questions. And when the same symbols or sensations return night after night, you'll know you're in dialogue.

Stichomancy

The practice of divining through random passages of text feels deceptively simple, but it can be deeply profound. This is a method especially useful when your spirit allies speak in metaphor, symbols, or are best accessed through language itself. To begin, choose a book that feels resonant. It doesn't have to be "spiritual"; you might be drawn to poetry, mythology, philosophy, or even an old journal of your own. The key is to use a book that holds some energetic weight for you.

Many people use the term bibliomancy interchangeably with stichomancy, and while the two are closely related, I've come to understand a subtle but important difference in my own practice. This distinction reflects my own experience; other traditions may use these terms differently. Some people use bibliomancy to describe any book-based divination, but the broader approach aligns more closely with what is traditionally called stichomancy. For me, bibliomancy is a form of divination that specifically uses sacred texts – such as the Bible, Qur'an, or other revered spiritual writings – to divine messages. Bibliomancy carries a formal or devotional tone and is usually practiced with deep reverence for the spiritual authority of the text.

Stichomancy is more expansive and intuitive. It's not limited to sacred books, nor does it require adherence to any doctrine or religious tradition. Stichomancy is about receiving messages through random lines of written word, whether from a spiritual book, a novel, a song lyric collection, or a dog-eared poetry anthology you've carried for years. In my work, stichomancy feels more like listening to a whisper hidden in plain sight, like spirit sliding a message under the door through the most unexpected lines of prose or verse.

For me, each serves a slightly different function. Bibliomancy might guide you when you need a spiritual anchor or a moral compass. Stichomancy, conversely, often speaks more fluidly to the symbolic, poetic, and personal. It allows spirit to communicate through a broader lens, through mystery, metaphor, and synchronicity. Both methods are valid. The key is in how you use them, and more importantly, how you listen.

To practice stichomancy, hold the book in your hands, breathe with it, and set your intention. You might ask:

> *"What do I need to see right now? What message is being sent from spirit? Where am I being guided?"*

Then close your eyes, flip the pages a few times, and let your finger land without trying to steer it. Open your eyes and read the passage. Trust what stands out first – whether it's a single sentence or entire paragraph. Allow it to work on you. Let it sink in and echo. Sometimes it will be direct. Other times, it's symbolic and requires unpacking. Sit with the passage. Journal what it means. Ask your guides to show you more if needed. This practice is especially effective during transitional times or when you need confirmation.

CLOSING RITUAL FOR DIVINATION

At the end of any session – drawing cards, asking yes/no pendulum questions, interpreting symbols in your environment, or receiving messages through dreams – it's vital to close the space. Thank the spirits. Clear your space. Ground your energy. Even if it feels like nothing big happened, the act of gratitude maintains the relationship. You might say:

"Thank you for your guidance. I honor what has been shared. I now close this space."

Making divination your own

In spirit work, divination is often the moment where the veil feels thinnest. It's a place of trust, not certainty. Some days, the answers are crystal clear. Other times, you'll be offered mystery, symbols that won't make sense until much later, signs that seem contradictory, or silence that asks you to wait. These are not failures of the tool. They're invitations into deeper listening.

We've covered several forms of divination in this chapter, from cartomancy and bibliomancy to pendulums and elemental signs. Every culture has its own traditions. Part of your work may be reclaiming or reviving the divinatory languages of your lineage. Do so with care and respect. With practice, these techniques can become a profound means of dialogue with guides or spirits you've built strong relationships with.

Divination is more than a tool for answers; it's a living relationship. It evolves with your practice, mirrors your growth, and reflects the way spirit chooses to engage with you. If there's one truth that holds across all traditions, it's that no tool works without the spirit of the practitioner being actively present. You aren't asking the universe to do the work for you, you're listening, participating, and co-creating.

You should never use divination to spy on others, manipulate outcomes, or seek validation that bypasses your own knowing. Spirit doesn't reward control. It responds to curiosity, humility, and heart. If you ever feel uncertain about using a tool, pause. Reflect. Ask if your intention is clean. Divination is powerful because it invites us to be honest with ourselves, spirit, and the energies we are co-weaving with.

Divination is a threshold. It's where the spiritual meets the symbolic, where you learn to read the world with more than just your eyes. It's not about collecting predictions but cultivating trust. The more you show up and do the work with sincerity, reverence, and openness, the more fluently the messages will come. Keep asking. Keep listening. Spirit is always speaking; you just have to learn how to hear it.

PRACTICE SUMMARY

- Pick one tool (cards, runes, pendulum) and dedicate a week to using it daily.
- Before asking big questions, practice with simple ones: "What energy surrounds me today?"
- Record your results, reflect, and write how accurate they feel afterward.
- Experiment with layering tools (such as pulling a card after pendulum work) and notice any new depths of insight.

CHAPTER 14

Calling and engaging spirits

The word "summon" tends to carry a dramatic weight, thanks in part to pop culture where summoning is often portrayed as an aggressive command, or as a means of calling something unknown into a ritual circle. In real spirit work, however, summoning is more nuanced.

To summon a spirit is to intentionally call it forth. This may take the form of an invocation, where the spirit is invited to merge more closely with your own energetic field, or an evocation, where the spirit is called into the space around you. The key differentiator is intent and relationship.

In my own practice, I rarely use the word "summon" because it can imply hierarchy or force. Spirit work thrives in mutual respect. I call. I invite. I make space. Spirits don't always show up just because we ask, and they certainly aren't beholden to us. That said, there are structured ways to summon with integrity, particularly when you've established rapport with a spirit.

You might choose to summon a spirit when:

- you've already worked with this spirit and have their permission

- you're entering sacred space and need their presence for a specific purpose (guidance, protection, healing, etc.)
- you're engaging in formal ritual work or trance practices that require a clear spiritual container
- you've created an altar, offerings, and protections appropriate to that spirit's nature.

Summoning without understanding is risky. Summon is about alignment, not dominance. Just because a spirit can be called doesn't mean it should be. Ethical spirit workers ask themselves: *Why this spirit? Why now? Have I prepared adequately? Have I attuned to their energy before making this call?* Before attempting to summon any spirit, attune to them first. Enter into meditation or communion. Leave offerings. Speak aloud:

> *"If it is in alignment, and you are willing,*
> *I invite you to be present with me now."*

Let it be a request, not a demand. If you receive signs of presence – shifts in air pressure, changes in your own intuitive state, an inner sense of recognition – continue with reverence. If not, accept the silence. Sometimes, the answer is "no."

More ceremonial paths to summoning, such as using sigils, sacred names, incense, planetary hours, or ritual tools, are best reserved for those trained in these systems. What matters most is that your request is rooted in clarity, sovereignty, and care.

Remember, spirit work is not a performance. Summoning is not a trick. It is a sacred conversation. Take your time learning the language. Rather than a set of rules, this chapter is meant to help you remember what you already know somewhere deep in your bones: you are not separate from spirit. You are part of the conversation. Whether you call it in or call it forth, the connection is already there. The work is simply to learn how to listen.

Summoning can be as simple as setting a clear call. Begin with protection in place, then speak aloud:

> *"Spirit ally of wisdom and compassion, I invite you to draw near if it is right and safe to do so."*

Listen for subtle shifts: a sensation in the room, a thought that doesn't feel your own, or an image that flashes across your mind. If nothing happens, don't be discouraged; sometimes the timing isn't right. If something does arrive, always close with gratitude and a clear dismissal such as: "Thank you for your presence. You may now depart in peace." Ending well is as important as beginning.

In spirit work, language shapes how we move through ritual and engage the unseen. Two terms often used, sometimes interchangeably, sometimes incorrectly, are "invocation" and "evocation." These aren't just technical words for ceremonial magicians or those deep into ritual magic. They are practical concepts that define how you interact with spiritual allies, ancestors, guides, and unknown or unfamiliar spirits.

Invocation or evocation?

Invocation is about calling a spirit inward, into yourself, your body, your consciousness. It's a form of embodiment. When you invoke, you're inviting the essence of a spirit or deity to move through you. This isn't possession in the Hollywood sense. It's more like shared space, allowing yourself to temporarily become a vessel for spirit's wisdom, power, presence, or guidance. Invocation can be subtle or intense.

Sometimes you'll speak differently. Other times a shift in posture or emotion lets you know something sacred has arrived. Invocation is sacred intimacy.

Evocation, on the other hand, is calling a spirit forward, into your space but not your body. You are summoning its presence, but you remain the anchor. The spirit might appear beside you, around you, or within the space you've created for it. This is a more common approach in mediumship or protective work, when you're in conversation with an ancestor, spirit guide, or maybe an entity that needs boundaries. Evocation creates a container where the spirit and practitioner are distinct but connected.

The difference matters. If you're working with a divine being, say a goddess or an archangel, you may choose invocation when you want to embody their traits, speak their messages, or channel healing. If you're working with an unfamiliar spirit, or one whose energy you're still learning, evocation allows for connection with more clarity and safety.

MY OWN EXPERIENCE

I've always approached these distinctions less from academic definition and more from experience.

Evocation came first, in my early days of mediumship. Spirits would appear beside me, offer impressions, or share images or words. They stayed distinct. I learned boundaries. I learned how to hold space without being consumed by it. Invocation came later, when the relationships were more anchored, more rooted in trust. That's often how it unfolds. You start with evocation: safe, clear, observational. And if the connection deepens, you might open the door to something more embodied.

I remember the first time I truly invoked. I wasn't attempting invocation in the ways I had read about or imagined, but I was standing at my altar, offering words of gratitude to a spirit with whom I'd built a deep, trusted relationship. Somewhere between the candle flicker and my whispered prayer, something shifted. My voice took on a rhythm that wasn't mine. A depth entered the room. My hands moved with intention I didn't plan. And when it was over, I cried, not from fear but recognition. Something sacred had moved through me.

Neither is better than the other. Both have their place. What matters is discernment: knowing what you're ready for; the nature of the spirit you're working with; and always anchoring in protection, clarity, and consent – yours and theirs.

Before either invocation or evocation, you need to prepare your space, your energy, and yourself. This isn't about elaborate set-dressing unless that helps you get into the right mindset. It's about creating alignment. You're entering sacred space, which begins with clarity.

Preparing to evoke or invoke

Start by checking in with yourself: *How am I arriving to this work today? Am I grounded? Am I emotionally regulated, or is something else pulling my focus?* If you're scattered, anxious, or angry, tend to that first. Take a walk, pull a few cards, light a candle, breathe. Spirit work amplifies what's already present, so it's essential to come into it as centered as possible.

From there, your physical space becomes the mirror of your inner one. You don't need a perfectly curated altar, though if you have one, beautiful. You just need intention. Tidy up. Light a bit of incense or use a cleansing herb you have on hand. Open a window or speak a few words aloud to claim the energy of the room. Something simple like:

> *"This is a space of clarity. All that is not in service to my highest good is released."*

Protection is essential. Whether you're calling a spirit in (invocation) or calling it forth into the room (evocation), you're opening a doorway. Not every spirit is harmful, but they're not all helpful either. Having boundaries in place is respectful. I always reinforce my personal energy before beginning; I imagine my field solid and luminous, like a sphere around me. I call in my guides or name the kind of energy I'm available for:

> *"Only those in alignment with love, truth, and mutual consent may enter this space."*

That kind of boundary keeps things clean. Now you can prepare for evocation or invocation:

- **Evocation** When preparing for evocation, you might create a physical boundary for the spirit's presence:

a circle, candlelit corner, or dedicated offering bowl or item. This is making space for them outside of you. I often place a chair or cushion opposite me, not because I expect a ghost to sit down, but because I'm signaling that I'm open to dialogue, not merging. Evocation is relational. It's a back-and-forth.

- **Invocation** This requires a different readiness. When you're calling a spirit or divine being into your energy, you're asking them to move through your body, your breath, your voice. This demands a high level of trust and deep grounding. I recommend doing some kind of anchoring practice before you begin: maybe breathwork, a centering mantra, or even a short chant that calls you fully into the present moment. You want to feel grounded before you open to anything beyond yourself.

You might also consider symbolic or physical preparation: wearing clothing or jewelry associated with the being you're invoking, anointing yourself with oil, or sitting in a pose of reverence. But again, these aren't rules, they're tools. Choose what brings you into right relationship.

Some spirits prefer one method over another. Some deities are rarely invoked; they remain external, powerful presences. Others crave direct embodiment. The same applies to guides and ancestors. Listen. Pay attention to how the spirit seems to respond when you approach. If you're unsure, start with evocation. Build the relationship there, from the edge of a threshold. Not every spirit needs to be invited in. Not every practitioner needs to act as a vessel. Your boundaries are sacred.

Embodiment and encounter

When spirit contact begins, you'll often feel a subtle shift before anything dramatic. It may begin as pressure behind the eyes, a change in temperature, or a prickle at the back of your neck. It might feel like someone just entered the room, even if you're alone. Your body knows before your mind catches up.

In evocation, the presence tends to feel near but not within. There's a sensation of "other," like a conversation across a threshold. The air might feel charged. You may hear or feel answers rather than thoughts of your own. Some people sense visual impressions, symbols, colors, or scents. Maybe your eyes are drawn to a corner of the room or an object that feels newly meaningful. In evocation, contact is relational: you stay in your body, and the spirit stays in theirs. You observe. You ask. You receive.

With invocation, the experience is more immersive. You may feel like being flooded from the inside: your breath shifts, your posture may subtly (or dramatically) change, your words may come with a different tone or cadence. Depending on the energy of the spirit, maybe you feel a surge of confidence, a heaviness in your limbs, or a lightness in your chest. Sometimes the experience is emotional: joy, grief, or fierceness rising without clear origin.

It's important to stay grounded in your own energy, even while sharing space with another. If something feels overwhelming, you can pause. You can name your limits aloud. You're not letting your body be overtaken, you're in partnership. If you ever feel a sharp internal "no," trust that.

Discernment is key. Just because something shows up doesn't mean it should stay. I've had moments where I thought I was invoking a particular ally, only to realize through how it felt in my body – tight, anxious, or suddenly confused – that I'd picked up something else. If that happens, stop, thank the energy for its time, and close the space. You can always try again later.

Pay attention to the differences. In evocation, you're more likely to receive information through external channels: cards, runes, pendulum movement, or auditory signs. In invocation, the answers tend to come from inside: gut responses, knowing without logic, words that tumble from your mouth before you've thought them. Neither is better than the other. One may come more naturally to you, or shift depending on the spirit or the season of your life.

If you ever feel unsure afterward – if you feel drained, emotionally tangled, or just off – it's okay to step back. Cleanse your space. Take a salt bath. Eat grounding food. Ask your trusted guides to clear away any lingering energy. Then reflect. Journal what you experienced, even if it didn't make sense. Spirit work is often mysterious in the moment, with meaning crystallizing with time.

Ultimately, invocation and evocation are practices of deep relationship. As well as tools to find answers or energy, they're ways of building sacred trust across the veil. That takes time, humility, and a willingness to keep showing up with curiosity and care. Opening to the spirit world is not just about access, but responsibility. When you begin invoking or evoking spirits, the door between realms becomes more porous. That doesn't mean you're at the mercy of anything that wanders through. You're the one setting the rules. You're the one holding the container.

PROTECT YOURSELF

Protection is not paranoia. It's wisdom. Just as you wouldn't invite a stranger into your home without boundaries, you don't invite spiritual energy into your body or space without clear terms. Before working with invocation or evocation, ask yourself:

- Do I know who I'm calling in?
- Have I set the space energetically?
- Do I trust my discernment enough to end it if something feels wrong?
- Do I have a grounding or clearing practice I can use afterward?

Your intention is the first line of protection. Speak it aloud or hold it firmly in your chest. You can say:

> *"I open this space for connection with [name or type of spirit], in alignment with my highest good and in the spirit of mutual respect. Nothing uninvited may remain."*
>
> Then build a protective container. That might look like casting a circle, lighting a candle, placing boundary crystals around your space, or playing a specific piece of music that energetically frames the session. These are cues to your body and the spirits that this is sacred work.

Ending a session

When your session ends, whether it felt deeply meaningful or simply quiet, it's vital to close the space. Speak your ending. Thank the spirit for their time and clearly state that they are now released. You might say something like:

> *"Thank you for your presence and wisdom. Our time together is complete. You may return to your realm in peace. This space is now closed."*

Then physically shift the energy. Blow out the candle. Ring a bell. Wash your hands. Shake out your body. Open a window. Take a few deep breaths and bring your awareness back into your surroundings. These simple actions signal to your nervous system that the ritual space is complete.

Integration is the final part of the work. Journal what you sensed, felt, or received, whether it was subtle or profound. Sometimes the messages don't land until days later. And even if "nothing" seemed to happen, you may notice shifts in your dreams, energy, or perception in the days that follow.

And if something feels off – lingering heaviness, disorientation, or unease – trust your discernment. Clear your space again. Use smoke, salt, sound, or prayer. Ask your spiritual allies to help reset the energy. Drink water. Get outside. Lay your body on the earth. Spirit work doesn't always tie itself up neatly with a bow, but you don't need to sit in discomfort to be "doing it right."

Remember, invocation and evocation aren't passive acts. They're relational practices that require your presence, awareness, and will. You're not surrendering your power. You're learning how to wield it in collaboration with spirit with purpose, with intention, and always with choice.

Choosing your method and moving forward

When it comes to deciding whether to bring forth a spirit or call it in, decide which is more aligned with your intention and capacity in the moment. Both approaches offer profound potential for connection, and require a level of awareness and responsibility.

Invocation may feel more intimate and personal. It invites the qualities, consciousness, or energy of a spirit into your own body or aura. It's well suited for times of transformation, ritual embodiment, deep communion, or when you're seeking to embody aspects of a being like courage, healing, or truth. It is especially resonant when working with ancestors, deities, or archetypal energies you trust and already have a relationship with.

Evocation, however, maintains a respectful distance. You're creating a space where the spirit may arrive and communicate without crossing into your field. It's useful in the early stages of building trust with a new guide, or when working with energies that feel powerful but not yet fully known. It also gives you a clearer sense of your own energy, allowing you to observe without becoming the channel.

You might begin with evocation to establish boundaries with spirit and gradually move into invocation as the relationship strengthens. Or you might alternate between them depending on the type of spirit you're working with, or the kind of guidance you're seeking. Spirit work is not static. It evolves.

What matters most is that your practice feels authentic. You don't have to speak with perfect poetic flair. You don't need elaborate rituals (unless you love them). You simply need clarity of purpose, a willingness to listen, and the ability to stay rooted in your own energy.

You'll learn through experience. Sometimes that learning will be messy. You might try invocation and feel overwhelmed. You might evoke and feel nothing. That's okay. There's no "right" way. There's just *your* way, refined over time. Keep notes. Stay curious. Check in with yourself. And trust that your spiritual allies are far more patient and loving than many people expect. They want to connect. They want to be honored, not feared. And they don't require perfection, they require presence.

If you're ever in doubt, return to the basics. Ground. Shield. Center. Ask clearly. Close your space when you're finished. Reflect. These simple practices are the backbone of spirit work and will carry you through every step of your evolution.

EXERCISE: Calling a spirit in

1. **Find a quiet and comfortable space.** Somewhere you can focus without interruption. Set the mood by lighting a candle, burning incense, or surrounding yourself with meaningful objects that resonate with the energy of the spirit you wish to invite. Breathe deeply and center yourself. Visualize roots growing from your body into the earth, anchoring you securely.
2. **Set your intention clearly.** Know who you wish to connect with and why. Consider researching the spirit beforehand. Understanding their associations, symbols, and energy will help you attune to their presence.
3. **Create a protective space.** Do this by visualizing a sphere of light around you. This sacred container helps to hold your energy and keeps the connection clear and safe. When you're ready, begin speaking to the spirit aloud or silently with sincerity. If invoking a goddess like Athena, for example, you might say:

   "Glorious Athena, wise and radiant, protector and strategist, I invite your presence with reverence and clarity. If you are willing, I welcome your guidance here."

4. **Speak slowly and from the heart.** Allow space for silence. Pay attention to any shifts: tingling, emotions, a wave of calm, or mental imagery. These may be signs the spirit is present. If it feels appropriate, speak to them.

Ask for insight or simply listen. The response may come in the form of thoughts, impressions, or inner knowing. Trust your own perception.

5. **Express your gratitude.** When the moment feels complete, offer thanks for any presence, insight, or guidance. Visualize the light around you gently dissolving and bring your awareness fully back into your body. Afterward, take time to reflect. Journal what you felt or received, even if it felt subtle. Each invocation deepens your relationship with spirit and strengthens your confidence in this work.

EXERCISE: Calling a spirit forth

This exercise is about calling a spirit to appear or make its presence known in a space outside of yourself. Approach this practice with clarity, preparation, and deep respect.

1. **Select a quiet, undisturbed space.** Cleanse the area physically and energetically. Try burning herbs, ringing a bell, sprinkling salt water, or any method that aligns with your practice. Set a clear intention: *Who am I calling, and why?* Beforehand, take time to learn about the spirit: their nature, domain, symbols, and any relevant history or cultural context.

2. **Create a defined sacred space.** Some practitioners cast a circle; others arrange candles, crystals, or items linked to the spirit being called. Visualize a protective boundary around this space and affirm that only spirits aligned with

your highest good may enter. First, call in your guides or protective allies. They are your spiritual support and will affirm your sovereignty during the work. Then, begin the evocation. Speak aloud or silently, inviting the spirit with words of respect and clarity. For example:

"Spirit of healing and restoration, if you are willing and aligned, I invite your presence into this space. May you come in peace, and may this be a moment of mutual understanding."

3. **Offer a symbolic gesture, such as water, flowers, or incense.** Offerings act as an energetic bridge. Be patient. Stay grounded in your body and hold the intention clearly. Remain aware of the atmosphere. Some spirits arrive with subtle shifts: air pressure, scent, emotion, or mental images. If you feel a presence, communicate with them respectfully. Ask questions or simply observe. Not all spirits will communicate directly; presence itself can be meaningful. Trust your intuition.
4. **Thank the spirit and release them.** When the encounter feels complete, speak aloud your gratitude and affirm that the connection is now closed. Dismantle the space gently and ground your energy; drink water, eat something, or take a moment outside.

Summoning is powerful work. As your confidence builds and your discernment sharpens, the process will become more fluid. Stay humble, stay respectful, and always remember: you are engaging in a relationship, not a transaction.

PRACTICE SUMMARY

» Begin with a clear protective practice before any summoning attempt.

» Start small: invite only benevolent, familiar spirits you've worked with before.

» Experiment with spoken invocation (calling) versus creating a space for evocation (inviting presence into the room). Always close with thanks and dismissal.

» Record your method, results, and how the spirit responded.

A final word

I hope you see how much of this path is already alive within you. Spirit work is not about memorizing rules or mastering techniques to perfection. It is about relationship, trust, and the willingness to step into connection with openness and respect.

Every exercise, ritual, and practice you explore is a tool to remind you of what you are capable of: listening deeply, discerning wisely, and standing firmly in your own integrity. No one else can define the way you walk this path. That is the gift and the responsibility of spirit work; it must be lived.

Trust yourself to know what feels right, and have the courage to walk away from what does not. Let discernment be your compass, intention your anchor, and integrity your guide. May your practice continue to evolve as a living dialogue with spirit. You are more prepared than you may realize, and the spirits will meet you in kind when you walk with authenticity.

Bibliography

Agrippa, Heinrich Cornelius. *Three Books of Occult Philosophy*. Translated by J. F. St. Paul, MN: Llewellyn Publications, 1993.

Barrett, David V. *The New Believers: A Survey of Sects, Cults and Alternative Religions*. London: Cassell, 2001.

Barrett, Francis. *The Magus: A Complete System of Occult Philosophy*. London: Lackington, Allen & Co., 1801.

Budge, E. A. Wallis. *Egyptian Magic*. Mineola, NY: Dover Publications, 1991.

Cavendish, Richard. *The Black Arts*. New York: G. P. Putnam's Sons, 1967.

Crowley, Aleister. *Magick in Theory and Practice*. York Beach, ME: Weiser Books, 1997.

Eason, Cassandra. *A Complete Guide to Psychic Development: 100 Ways to Tap into Your Psychic Potential*. Berkeley, CA: Crossing Press, 2003.

Fortune, Dion. *Psychic Self-Defense*. York Beach, ME: Weiser Books, 2001.

Greer, John Michael. *The Encyclopedia of Natural Magic*. St. Paul, MN: Llewellyn Publications, 2005.

Harner, Michael. *The Way of the Shaman*. New York: HarperOne, 1990.

Huson, Paul. *Mastering Witchcraft: A Practical Guide for Witches, Warlocks, and Covens*. New York: Perigee, 1970.

Illes, Judika. *The Element Encyclopedia of 5,000 Spells*. London: HarperElement, 2004.

Illes, Judika. *Encyclopedia of Spirits: The Ultimate Guide to the Magic of Fairies, Genies, Demons, Ghosts, Gods & Goddesses*. New York: HarperOne, 2009.

Kelly, Aidan A. *Eros and Touch from a Pagan Perspective: Divided for Love's Sake*. Eugene, OR: Pickwick Publications, 2014.

Lévi, Éliphas. *Transcendental Magic: Its Doctrine and Ritual*. Translated by A. E. Waite. York Beach, ME: Weiser Books, 2001.

Mathers, S. L. MacGregor, trans. *The Key of Solomon the King (Clavicula Salomonis)*. York Beach, ME: Weiser Books, 2000.

Melton, J. Gordon, ed. *Encyclopedia of Occultism and Parapsychology*. 2 vols. Farmington Hills, MI: Gale Group, 2001.

Morrison, Dorothy. *Everyday Magic: Spells and Rituals for Modern Living*. St. Paul, MN: Llewellyn Publications, 2001.

Penczak, Christopher. *Spirit Allies: Meet Your Team from the Other Side*. Woodbury, MN: Red Wheel/Weiser, 2002.

Regardie, Israel. *The Golden Dawn: The Original Account of the Teachings, Rites, and Ceremonies of the Hermetic Order*. St. Paul, MN: Llewellyn Publications, 1999.

Soca, Gabriel. "What are Starseeds and How to Know if You Are One?" *Gaia*, accessed November 15, 2020. https://www.gaia.com/article/am-i-a-starseed-types-characteristics

Summers, Montague. *The History of Witchcraft and Demonology*. Mineola, NY: Dover Publications, 2000.

Tyson, Donald. *Grimoire of the Necronomicon*. St. Paul, MN: Llewellyn Worldwide, 2008.

Valiente, Doreen. *An ABC of Witchcraft Past and Present*. Phoenix, AZ: Phoenix Publishing, 1988.

Waite, Arthur Edward. *The Book of Ceremonial Magic*. York Beach, ME: Weiser, 1999.

About the author

Sirian Shadow is a versatile and multifaceted practitioner, psychic, and author who provides spiritual guidance for empowerment and transformation. His mission is to inspire wisdom and empower personal and spiritual truth. He is the author of *Spirit World* and the oracles *Shadow of Darkness* and *Earth and Bone.*

sirianshadow

Also by Sirian Shadow

SPIRIT WORLD

Guides, ancestors, entities

ISBN: 9781922468413